Come, Let Us CELEBRATE!

Creative Celebrations of Reconciliation

by
Sarah O'Malley, O.S.B.
Robert Eimer, O.M.I.

Published by
Resource Publications, Inc.
160 E. Virginia St. Suite 290
San Jose, CA 95112

Prayer excerpt reprinted with permission from *Prayers for the Domestic Church: A Handbook for Worship in the Home* by Rev. Edward M. Hays (1979: Forest of Peace Books, Inc. Easton, Ks 66020).

Scripture text used in this work are taken from the NAB, copyright © 1970, by the Confraternity of Christian Doctrine, Washington, D.C., and are used by permission of the copyright owner. All rights reserved.

SPIRIT OF THE LIVING GOD, by Daniel Iverson. Copyright © 1935, 1963. Moody Press. Moody Bible Institute of Chicago. Used by permission.

Editorial Director: Kenneth Guentert
Production Editor: Scott Alkire
Mechanical Layout: Sharon Montooth
Cover Design: Christine Benjamin

ISBN 0-89390-082-6
Library of Congress Catalog Card Number 86-060168
Printed and bound in the United States 5 4 3 2

*To a pastoral leader, Bishop Paul Anderson,
who saw his mission in the Duluth Diocese
as one of "reconciliation of people to God
and one another." His support of our
parish ministry will never be forgotten.*

Contents

Acknowledgments

We are sincerely grateful to all who participated in the preparation of these communal celebrations.

First of all we thank Fr. Roger Schoenhofen, O.M.I., Sr. Elaine Jost, O.S.B., but especially Fr. Bob Moosbrugger, O.M.I., and Barbara West for their pioneer work with reconciliation services on the West End.

Second, we thank Carol and John Wabik for their creativity and their timeless labor in creating the liturgical decor for our services.

Third, we are grateful for the music ministry provided by our youth choir under the leadership of Dawn Fausz, Kevin Harrington, Clyde Jago and Dick Frost.

Fourth, we thank Mother Grace Marie Braun, O.S.B., and Fr. Don Bargen, O.M.I., our religious superiors, for their encouragement in writing this book.

Fifth, we thank Pat Thul for the lovely calligraphy work she did for the parish.

Sixth, we thank Fr. Ron Brassard for his assistance in expanding the list of appropriate songs.

Finally, we thank the parishoners of Holy Family Catholic Parish. Most of the religious articles distributed to the congregation were assembled by the elderly in the parish. Others volunteered their time as lectors or liturgical assistants. The list is too large to name each individually, but we cannot omit the names of Frank Bourassa, Sr. Pauline Micke, O.S.B., Ginny Lind, Charles House, Carol Mlodozyniec, Jan Pilon, Lois Jackson, Mario Schinigoi, and Barbara Reynolds.

Preface

The new Rite of Penance (now not really all that new) with its stated and implied demands for new penitential space, new pastoral skills, new ritual for all involved, can lead us to concentrate on the more superficial aspects of the rite. The beauty of this book is that it seems to arise from insights nearer to the heart of the revised ritual.

As sacrament, the church has the duty to show in its life those signs which speak most clearly the Gospel. Therefore, we are a community which celebrates who we are: people washed, people fed, people called, people healed. But these signs, ritualized in sacrament, gain their authenticity only in so far as they reflect our life — or, at least, the life we are striving in grace to live. In other words, our sacramental life lifts up in sign our daily communal and individual lives. To be authentic, a sacrament arises from an environment which it reflects; our common and individual Christian lives provide the only soil suitable for the nurture and emergence of our sacramental life. Briefly put — you can only preach authentically what you practice.

So the sacrament of Penance arises from the church's life of penance. Much more than did the old rite, the revised one captures this. Most significantly it witnesses to this in its recognition that sin is a condition of individuals, communities and the world at large. With its emphasis on shared prayer, scripture, and the communal setting, the present rite situates the celebration of Penance in the context of the church's *life of penance.* Thus, our sacrament of Penance becomes linked (even if only subtly) to our life of penance: our fasting, our daily prayer, our almsgiving, our seeking after peace and justice.

Another important nuance of the new rite is its thrust. Both catechesis for and celebration of the old rite carried with it a backward-leaning notion. We "went to confession" primarily to restore ourselves to our baptismal "state" of sanctifying grace. This is certainly true. But it is just as certainly not the whole truth. The purpose of penance is not only restoration of a state of grace but, equally, growth in grace — movement toward something beyond; movement to new insight, new action, new behaviors, all founded on a deeper consciousness of who we are *called to become.* The revised rituals carry this weight far more effectively for "pew people" than did the old rite.

Because the celebrations designed in this collection seem (by intent, Providence or both) to capture more of the *heart* of the new rite of Penance I recommend them highly; but with a caution, which I know is shared by the designers. During your preparations, allow yourselves to enter into them. Do not simply use them. Adapt where necessary for your community. But most important, see them as an extension of your community's life of penance. Let them serve as both a celebration of who you are but let them serve as a call to what you can be. Let them both speak and shape the Body of Christ.

Ed Murray

Introduction

In many Catholic churches in the United States today, there are diminishing lines of penitents outside the confessional room on Saturday afternoon. Many reasons have been given for this phenomenon: a new understanding of sin and the ways sin can be forgiven outside the confessional; the decline of the "devotional" weekly confession; the inadequacy felt by priest and penitent with the revised rite; and an insufficient explanation of the new penitential rite.

On the other hand, communal reconciliation services became popular in the Seventies. Instead of lines of silent people outside a confessional, we witnessed hundreds of people actively participating in the various steps of the sacrament: making an examination of conscience and an act of sorrow together, and reciting a common penance.

The Roman Rite calls confession the "Rite of Penance" and the "Rite for Reconciliation." For the sake of clarity, we will subsequently refer to confession as "Communal Reconciliation."

The popularity of Communal Reconciliation is no doubt more than a passing fad; instead it is a "sign of the times." Today, Catholics are finding a meaning in the celebration of Communal Reconciliation which they may not presently be finding in private confession. In the church's renewal of all the sacraments, the "communal dimension" is being emphasized. "It is to be stressed that whenever rites, according to their specific nature, make provision for communal celebration involving the presence and active participation of people, this way of celebrating is to be preferred, so far as possible, to a celebration that is individual and quasi-private (No. 24, *Constitution of the Sacred Liturgy*)." It is precisely this active participation of the community which makes Communal Reconciliation such a poignant and life-giving spiritual experience.

We are not denying the value of the private form of reconciliation. Pope John Paul II in a recent document on "Reconciliation and Penance" emphasized the value of the private form. Yet even John Paul II, in that document, highlights also the value of the communal elements in Form II.

> The second form of celebration, precisely by its specific dimension, highlights certain aspects of great importance: the word of God listened to in common has a remarkable effect as compared to its individual reading and better emphasizes the ecclesial character of conversion and reconciliation. It is particularly meaningful at various seasons of the liturgical year and in connection with events of special pastoral importance. The only point that needs mentioning here is that for celebrating the second form there should be an adequate number of confessors present.
>
> (Apostolic Exhortation on Reconciliation and Penance)

However, our concern in this book is to present creative ways of celebrating "Communal Reconciliation." Communal Reconciliation is an appropriate term because it emphasizes the communal dimension of the sacrament, as the *Constitution of the Sacred Liturgy* exhorts us to do.

There is a unique power found in the language and use of symbols. One rich heritage of the Catholic Church is her respect for and use of symbols in her liturgy. Tapping that heritage, these penitential rites lean heavily on symbol and symbolic action in order to reinforce the themes.

Some of the symbols used in the reconciliation services are familiar ones that people will easily identify — water, candles, oil. Other symbols, though familiar and traditional, are used in an unfamiliar way — for instance, the use of a rock as a symbol of Christ. Finally, some symbols are not as common — such as the use of paper dragons. We have tried to use the old symbols creatively and to develop an awareness of new symbols which may be less familiar but are nevertheless very rich in meaning.

Yet with all our efforts to be creative, we hope we have avoided being gimicky. Since Jesus is the Healer and Forgiver through his Spirit, we realize that the first requirement for an effective Communal Reconciliation is an atmosphere of faith, humility and prayer. Even the finest liturgy, technically speaking, would be shallow and empty if faith and humility were absent. Thus, we presuppose that every effort will have been made to create within the congregation an attitude of interior faith, prayerfulness and humility. But given that, we also believe there is a power in good preparation, in the use of clear and strong symbols, and in a sense of unity that comes from cohesive themes.

Other elements of the service cannot be overlooked. Suitable music, a judicious choice of scripture passages, light, color, and decor all serve to highlight the theme and the symbols. Since we are convinced that Communal Reconciliations provide "teachable moments," the homily becomes very important in explaining the interrelationship of the readings, the symbols, the theme and the celebration of reconciliation.

There is a predictable pattern in these communal celebrations. Certain elements generally appear in the same order: an introduction, the liturgy of the Word, a homily, an examination of conscience, an act of sorrow, the symbolic action and confession by the penitent, a sign of peace, the absolution or blessing by the priest or priests, and the designation of a common penance. This pattern has given penitents a "touchstone of familiarity," not unlike the traditional "five steps for a good confession" found in the *Baltimore Catechism*.

This collection has a special advantage: all of the celebrations have been used in a parish setting and have been tested for their effectiveness. In the mid-Seventies, we began to use these services in Holy Family Parish in preparation for the major feasts of Christmas and Easter. Later we extended them beyond Christmas and Easter, providing a communal celebration in the fall around the Feast of All Saints and one preceding the Feast of Pentecost.

Of course, many of these communal services can be used for any occasion and are not necessarily linked to any particular feast.

These communal reconciliation services are adapted for use in Form II, with several priests giving absolution or in Form III (general absolution in case of pastoral necessity) or, finally, in penitential celebrations as paraliturgies of reconciliation. Penitential celebrations are not sacramental; yet their value is to instill the proper dispositions in preparing people of all ages for the sacrament of Reconciliation. Penitential celebrations would certainly be appropriate for the beginning of Advent and the Lenten season; for a mission or retreat experience; or as part of the catechesis in preparing children for confession, or catechumens in the RCIA process. In addition, these services are very appropriate for youth retreats or seasonal communal celebrations for parochial schools or schools of religious education. A slight change in vocabulary and an adaption of the homily is all that is needed. Finally the rites of penitential celebration are very useful (as the *Rite of Penance* says) in places where no priest is available to give sacramental absolution.

The first sixteen services are complete with suggestions for music, with homily hints and an examination of conscience. The rituals can be used just as they are or be adapted, depending on the circumstances or on the needs of the parish or group. For those concerned about the length of the service, these communal celebrations were generally planned to be no more than one hour long. The remaining thirteen services need to be developed according to the taste and resources available to the planner.

We encourage liturgy planners to be creative in adapting these communal services for their congregation. We had been blessed in our parish with several gifted parishioners who have a talent for the use of color and decor. We generally gave some kind of religious article to the congregation to reinforce the theme of the service and to extend the symbol of forgiveness to the home. These articles were usually made by the elderly and homebound at a minimal cost. We highly recommend that assistant lay ministers hand out the articles after the penitents present themselves to the priest for the absolution or the imposition of hands. When we distributed the individual articles, we suggested that people hang them on the Christmas tree or in their home somewhere as a reminder of God's healing forgiveness. Drawing on the talents of many, we have allowed the power of symbol, color, and decor, music and action, to open the hearts of penitents and invite the gentle touch of the Spirit to forgive and heal.

Although the first sixteen services are divided into four categories, the divisions are not hard and fast. With minimal adaption, the services can be used for any season. This is especially true of the services listed as General, many of which were used for Advent or Lent.

The skeletal themes for the remaining thirteen services are not divided according to the liturgical season. The appropriateness of the choice of theme for the liturgical season is up to the planner's discretion.

Most of the music suggested is available from North American Liturgy Resources (10802 N. 23rd Ave, Phoenix, AZ 85029), specifically from the *Glory and Praise* songbooks. We have indicated other publishers in parentheses.

Part I
Advent

Theme: From the Tree of Death to the Tree of Life

Dominant Symbols: *Christmas Tree and "Oplatek"*

"This is my body which is for you." (1 Cor. 11:24) In the sanctuary the decor is dominated by two trees. To the left is a small, leafless dead tree in a stand. A prop resembling a serpent can be placed in its branches. To the right is a Christmas tree of similar size decorated with round white cardboard ornaments to represent large white hosts in the French tradition. The homily must emphasize the difference between the fruits of the tree of death in paradise and the fruits of new life from the cross, represented obliquely by the Christmas tree.

I. Introduction (*Remain seated*)

Priests enter quietly and take their places along with the lectors. People remain seated as the candles are lit. As the candles are lit the choir sings, "Prepare Ye the Way of the Lord" from *Godspell*, Stephen Schwartz.

A. Opening Prayer (*Stand*)

PRIEST: "Let us pray. O Lord Jesus Christ, who by dying on the tree of the cross overcame the death of sin caused by our first parents' eating of the forbidden tree of paradise, grant, we ask You, the abundant graces of your Nativity, that we may so live as to be worthy living branches of Yourself, the good and ever green Olive Tree, and in thy strength bear the fruit of good works for eternal life. Who lives and reigns for ever and ever."

ALL: Amen

B. Introduction to Scriptural Readings: (*Sit*)

In one sense we are children of Adam and Eve and because of that we have all tasted the fruit of death. But we are redeemed children of God, brothers and sisters of Christ, the second Adam. We have tasted of the fruit of another tree — the cross — the tree of life. In a way the story of salvation is the story of two trees, the tree of death in the Garden of Eden and the tree of life — the cross of Good Friday.

II. Liturgy of the Word:

A. Scriptural Mosaic from the Old and New Testament read by three lectors. (Short silence following readings.)

2

LEADER: And now let us listen to the story of our salvation: Beginning with the story of the First Adam and Eve as it is told to us in the book of Genesis.

READER 3: Then God said: "Let us make man in our image, after our likeness. Let them have dominion over the fish of the sea, the birds of the air and the cattle and over all the wild animals and all the creatures that crawl on the ground." (Gn. 1:26)

READER 2: God created man in his image . . . male and female, he created them. (Gn. 1:27)

READER 1: Then the Lord God planted a garden in Eden, in the east, and he placed there the man whom he had formed. Out of the ground the Lord God made various trees grow that were delightful to look at and good for food . . . (Gn. 2:8-9)

READER 3: The Lord God gave man this order: "You are free to eat from any trees in the garden except the tree of knowledge of good and bad. From that tree you shall not eat; the moment you eat from it, you are surely doomed to die." (Gn. 2:16-17)

READER 1: Now the serpent was the most cunning of all the animals that the Lord God had made. The serpent asked the woman, "Did God really tell you not to eat fom any of the trees in the garden?" (Gn. 3:1)

READER 2: "We may eat of the fruit of the trees in the garden; it is only about the fruit of the tree in the middle of the garden that God said, 'You shall not eat it or even touch it, lest you die,'" (Gn. 3:2-3)

READER 1: "You certainly will not die. No, God knows well that the moment you eat of it, you will be like gods who know what is good and what is bad." (Gn. 3:4-5)

READER 2: The woman saw that the tree was good for food, pleasing to the eyes and desirable for gaining wisdom. She took some of its fruit and ate it; and she also gave some to her husband, who was with her, and he ate it. Then the eyes of both of them were opened, and they realized they were naked; so they sewed fig leaves together and made loin cloths for themselves. (Gn. 3:6-7)

READER 3: The Lord God then called to the man and asked him, "Where are you?" (Gn. 3-9)

READER 1: "I heard you in the garden; but I was afraid because I was naked; so I hid myself." (Gn. 3-10)

READER 3: "Who told you that you were naked? You have eaten, then, from the tree of which I had forbidden you to eat." (Gn. 3-11)

READER 3: The Lord God then asked the woman, "Why did you do such a thing?" (Gn. 3:13)

READER 2: "The serpent tricked me into it; so I ate it." (Gn. 3:13)

READER 3: Then the Lord God said to the serpent: "Because you have done this . . . on your belly shall you crawl . . . I will put enmity between you and the woman and between your offspring and hers; He will strike at your head while you strike at his heel." (Gn. 3:14-15)

READER 1: And thus man disobeyed God and ate the forbidden fruit.

READER 2: And Adam and Eve tasted death because they had disobeyed.

READER 3: And Cain killed his brother Abel, and tasted the sin of murder.

READER 1: People built a tower of Babel, and there was pride and disunity and bitter arguments and struggles.

READER 2: And there were unnatural sins in the city of Sodom and Gommorah.

READER 3: And down through the ages the sons and daughters of Adam and Eve tasted the forbidden fruit of sin.

READER 1: But there was the *promise* . . .

READER 2: *The promise* of the redeemer . . .

READER 3: The promise of a Second Adam who would strike at the serpent's head as the serpent struck at his heel.

READER 1: And the day came to pass when The Second Adam arrived . . .

READER 2: A reading from the Holy Gospel according to Luke:

In those days Caesar Augustus published a decree ordering a census of the whole world. This first census took place while Quirinius was governor of Syria. Everyone went to his own town to register. So Joseph went from Nazareth in Galilee to Judea to David's town of Bethlehem — because he was of the house and lineage of David — to register with Mary, his espoused wife, who was with child.

While they were there the days of her confinement were completed. She gave birth to her first-born son and wrapped him in swaddling clothes and laid him in a manger, because there was no room for them in the place where the travelers lodged. (Lk. 2, 1-7)

READER 3: And the child grew up, and on Good Friday, He faced another tree, the tree of the cross. And He obeyed the father, and accepted the cross and was nailed to it. And Jesus, the Savior, asked us to remember the tree of the cross and to remember this obedience to the Father and this love for all of us.

READER 1: A reading from the first letter of Paul to the Corinthians.

I received from the Lord what I handed on to you, namely that the Lord Jesus on the night in which he was betrayed took bread, and after he had given thanks, broke it and said, "This is my body which is for you. Do this in remembrance of me." In the same way, after the supper, he took the cup, saying, "This cup is the new covenant in my blood. Do this, whenever you drink it, in remembrance of me." Every time, then, you eat this bread and drink this cup, you proclaim the death of the Lord until he comes! (1 Cor. 11:23-26) (Pause)

READER 2: And from this tree of the cross came a life-giving fruit. From this tree came the life of grace and from this tree came the Eucharist, the body and blood of Jesus Christ. And from this tree came a new promise. (Pause)

READER 3: A reading from the Gospel of John:

Jesus said to them, "Let me solemnly assure you, if you do not eat the flesh of the Son of Man and drink his blood you will have no life in you. He who feeds on my flesh and drinks my blood has life eternal, and I will raise him up on the last day." (Jn. 6:53-54)

B. Homily Hints:

1. The Old Testament begins with the story of Adam and Eve and the tree of paradise that becomes a tree of death:

- Adam and Eve say "No" to God in disobedience.

- Our first parents experience sin and death, the fruits of the tree of death.

2. Jesus, the Second Adam, becomes identified with another kind of tree, the Cross, which becomes the tree of life.

- From *this* tree came grace and life, the sacraments of Baptism and Eucharist (found symbolically in Jn. 19:31-37).

- An ancient tradition says that the cross was implanted in the place where Adam was buried; that Jesus' blood fell and touched the remains of the first Adam and redeemed Him.

3. Everything in the New Testament is written in the light of the paschal mystery.

- Christ's death and resurrection

- The nativity is not just a romantic story

- Already the cross hovered over Jesus in the slaughter of the innocents.

4. On Christmas, we emphasize the Christmas tree. Christmas tradition in certain countries hint at the "Christmas tree" being a symbol of the redeeming cross.

● We talked of the fruit of the tree of the cross being life and life-giving sacraments like the Eucharist.

● The French decorate the Christmas tree with white wafers, a symbol of the Eucharist. They make a link between the fruit of the Christmas tree and the fruit of the cross, the Eucharist.

5. What about us? What does all this have to do with the Sacrament of Reconciliation?

● We have tasted of the fruit of death since we have all sinned in the sin of the First Adam (original sin). Likewise we all share in the fruit of the cross, the tree of life through the sacraments, especially Baptism, the Eucharist and Reconciliation.

● Tonight we consciously come to the Second Adam to share of the fruit of the Cross — salvation, redemption, reconciliation.

6. After the reconciliation rite, (confession, absolution) we are giving you a symbol of Christmas along with a piece of Polish wafer. The Polish have a tradition of sharing white, unleavened bread at Christmas time. Our Reconciliation Service is a preparation for our Christmas Eucharist — tonight's symbol reminds us of Christ-Mass!

7. Included with that symbol is a blessing of the Christmas tree.

● You may have your tree up already but haven't blessed it.

● Let your tree remind you of the "tree of life", the cross, with its life-giving fruit, the sacraments.

III. Examination of Conscience:

LEADER: Lord, we have tasted the fruits of the forbidden tree. For the times we may have felt pride and bragged loudly and strutted like a peacock . . . (pause)

ALL: Lord, forgive us our sins.

LEADER: For the times we may have coveted material things and cheated or stolen or lied to acquire money and possessions . . . (pause)

ALL: Lord, forgive us our sins.

LEADER: For the times we may have desired pleasure selfishly, desired sex without commitment or responsibility . . . (pause)

ALL: Lord, forgive us our sins.

LEADER: For the times we may have become uncontrollably angry and allowed our anger to turn into hatred and revenge . . . (pause)

ALL: Lord, forgive us our sins.

LEADER: For the times we may have eaten gluttonously and drank too much, with little concern about the welfare of our bodies . . . (pause)

ALL: Lord, forgive us our sins.

LEADER: For the times we may have been envious of other's talents or good looks or good fortune . . . (pause)

ALL: Lord, forgive us our sins.

LEADER: For the times we have been lazy . . . lazy at work or at home, lazy in regard to worship or prayer . . . (pause)

ALL: Lord, forgive us our sins.

LEADER: Lord, we have tasted the fruits of sin. Now let us taste forgiveness in this sacrament of Reconciliation; let us taste of your love in the Christmas communion we shall receive; let us taste of the fruits of the Spirit; love, joy, peace, patience, kindness, goodness, faithfulness, humility,, and self-control. We ask this through Christ, the Second Adam, our Savior. Amen.

ALL SING: (Stand) "Come, O Lord" by Balhoff, Daigle, Ducote (refrain only).

IV. Sign of Sorrow *(Kneel)*

ALL: (Prayer of St. Francis) Lord, make me an instrument of your peace. Where there is hatred, let me sow love; where there is injury, pardon; where there is doubt, faith; where there is despair, hope; where there is darkness, light; where there is sadness, joy. O Divine Master, grant that I may seek not so much to be consoled, as to console; to be understood as to understand; to be loved, as to love; for it is in giving that we receive; it is in pardoning that we are pardoned; it is in dying that we are born to eternal life.

V. Blessing of the Symbol and Absolution *(Remain seated)*

A. Blessing of symbol and tree (incense)

"Lord of the forest, Maker of trees, we honor You as we dedicate this tree that it be a sign of Christmas. Green as life are its needled leaves; open and inviting are its outstretched branches; strong as love is its trunk. May we eat their fruit. May all trees be for us Christmas trees and trees of life. As redeemed sons and daughters of Adam and Eve, let us rejoice in this tree of Life; may the spirit of kindness and love rest upon it. Amen." *Prayers For the Domestic Church* by Edward Hays.

B. We invite each person to come forward down the center aisle to allow him or her to confess or receive absolution, or, if non-sacramental penitential celebration is used, to allow the priest to impose hands on the heads of each penitent.

VI. Common Penance:

We ask each person to do an act of charity before Christmas — for instance, to write a Christmas card, or visit a relative or shut-in, etc.

VII. Blessing of Each Other:

While the choir moves down the main aisle, we ask everyone to turn toward the center aisle.

A. The choir will sing through once the song of blessing: "The Peace of the Lord" by Gary Ault.

B. Then the congregation with one hand extended repeats the song of blessing.

C. Finally both choir and congregation sing the song.

VIII. Concluding Song:

"Lift up Your Hearts" by Roc O'Connor, S.J.

Suggestions:

1. The "oplatek" (Polish Christmas wafers) can be purchased inexpensively at the following address:

Franciscan Publishers
Franciscan Center
Pulaski, WI 54162

If you do not wish to use Polish Christmas wafers, any form of bread will do

2. The symbol is made from 3" x 6" red construction paper with green tree-shaped construction paper stapled to it. On the front are the words — "The tree of life — Taste its fruit," a crib and white host is sketched on the front. The tree forms a pocket for the "oplatek" and the "Blessing for the Christmas tree." A green pipe cleaner is attached at the top of the symbol so it can be hung like an ornament on their Christmas tree.

3. The following appropriate songs could be used for this service:
"Dwelling Place" by John Foley, S.J.
"Wood Hath Hope" by John Foley, S.J.
"Awake, O Sleeper" by Balhoff, Ducote, Daigle
"The Dawn of Day" by Lucien Deiss

COMMUNAL RECONCILIATION SERVICE NUMBER 2

Theme: The Father's Gift of Love

Dominant Symbol: *The Word of God*

"For while the law was given through Moses, this enduring love came through Jesus Christ." (Jn. 1:17)

Spotlights are focused on a wooden structure similar to a Christmas tree. On the wooden outline of the Christmas tree live Christmas tree branches are nailed. The idea is to create a kind of tabernacle that is similar to a Christmas tree. The structure, which can be decorated with Christmas lights, should be triangular and within it a manger with straw is placed. On the straw, a large Bible will be placed. Above the wooden structure hangs a mobile, composed of empty boxes wrapped with Christmas paper.

I. Introduction:

A. Lector reads the theme: "Forgiveness is a *gift* just as faith and salvation are gifts. We learn from the Bible that Jesus is a *gift* of love, the source of forgiveness, faith and salvation. Jesus, the Word made flesh, *is our Christmas gift*, Who continues to offer us forgiveness and salvation."

B. The ministers assemble in the rear of the church as the choir begins singing in a low tone: "Come, O Lord" by Balhoff, Ducote, Daigle.

As the choir sings, two candle-bearers, from the sacristy, bring candlebras and place them on stands next to the wooden structure. After the choir finishes singing, a group of three do a choral reading from John 1:1-5. After the first reading, the choir repeats the refrain of "Come, O Lord." As the choir sings, an incense bearer comes from the sacristy, bows to the center of the altar in front the manger and then stands to the left of the manger. The choral readers now read John 1:6-9. Then the choir again repeats the same refrain, and a person bearing a Bible comes from the sacristy, bows to the center and takes a position on the right of the manger facing the congregation. The choral readers then read John 1:10-13. The choir now repeats the refrain once more while the priests walk down the center aisle. After the song, one of the priests goes up to the incensor and puts incense in. He then walks over to the person with the Bible and incenses the Bible. Returning the incense to the incense-bearer, he takes the bible and places it with dignity on the straw of the manger. Then the incensor and book-bearer leave and the priests take their seats on the side of the pulpit. Then the whole congregation sings the refrain once more.

II. Opening Prayer:

LEADER: "Heavenly Father, the giver of all gifts, You gave on Christmas your greatest Gift, your only Son. Through Jesus, the Word, we experience your unconditional love. Through Jesus, we receive your gift of forgiveness and salvation. We ask this through Christ our Lord."

PEOPLE: Amen.

III. Liturgy of the Word:

A. Romans 5:15-21: (Paul contrasts our sin in Adam and Eve with the gracious gift of Jesus who is the second Adam.)

B. Sing refrain: "Glory and Praise to Our God" by Dan Schutte, S.J.

C. Matthew 1:18-21: (The angel announces to Joseph that Jesus will save his people from sin.)

D. Homily Hints:

1. Jesus is the Word of God made incarnate. He is present now in the Bible, the Word of God. That's why we placed the Bible in the manger to symbolize Christ, the Word, present among us tonight.

2. We think of Christmas as a time of giving gifts and in a way God is "Eternal Christmas" because He is the eternal gift-giver. That's the way God is since He is infinite love.

3. However, God's greatest gift is the gift of his Son, the source of most other gifts.

4. Jesus came bearing gifts from his Father: the gift of adoption, the gift of forgiveness, the gift of the Eucharist, etc.

5. Yet those gifts had a price tag — Jesus died for us.

6. In the T.V. program, "The Price is Right," there are conditions for receiving gifts. You have to guess a price, and if the price is right, you win. But God doesn't call us down and ask us to enter a game of chance. All He asks us to do is to recognize our sinfulness and receive the gift of forgiveness.

7. Are you willing to come down to the Savior as the shepherds and the magi did to receive the gift of forgiveness.

IV. Examination of Conscience:

Introduced by the leader to which the people respond, "Lord, we ask your forgiveness."

LEADER: *For the gift of freedom to worship* . . . For the times I have missed Mass because of laziness and negligence . . . (Pause)

ALL: Lord, we ask your forgiveness.

LEADER; *For the gift of parents and authority* . . . For the times I have failed to honor my parents or respect those in authority . . . (Pause)

ALL: Lord, we ask your forgiveness.

LEADER: *For the gift of life* . . . For the times I failed to take care of my health or threatened life wth hatred or violence . . . (Pause)

ALL: Lord, we ask your forgiveness.

LEADER: *For the gift of free speech* . . . For the times I misused the gift of speech through slander or angry and harsh words . . . (Pause)

ALL: Lord, we ask your forgiveness.

LEADER: *For the gift of possessions* . . . For the times I became greedy or the times I stole or cheated . . . (Pause)

ALL: Lord, we ask your forgiveness.

LEADER: *For the gift of pleasure* . . . For the times I was undisciplined and abused God's gift of pleasure in eating or drinking or sexual abuse . . . (Pause)

ALL: Lord, we ask your forgiveness.

LEADER: *For the gift of faith* . . . For the times I neglected my faith life, neither praying nor nourishing it with the sacraments . . . (Pause)

ALL: Lord, we ask your forgiveness.

LEADER: *For the gift of the Eucharist* . . . For the times I neglected the Eucharist or received Holy Communion with lukewarmness or lack of love . . . (Pause)

ALL: Lord, we ask your forgiveness.

V. Sign of Sorrow:

Kneel and make an act of sorrow together.

"Lord, all is gift — the faith to believe in your forgiveness and the forgiveness itself. We come to You with humility, to confess to you, and to the whole church of our brothers and sisters that we have sinned by abusing your gifts or by refusing them. We ask mercy, healing and forgiveness. We ask You, Lord, to give us this day the wisdom and courage to begin anew. Amen."

VI. Receiving The Symbol of Reconciliation and Absolution:

A. A priest asks each person to come to the front step in the middle aisle. A priest removes the open Bible from the manger and places it on a stand by the front step. The penitents first touch the Bible as a symbol of surrender to our Savior. Then they go to the priest on either side to confess and receive absolution; or if a non-sacramental penitential celebration is used, the priest imposes hands on each penitent.

B. Then the penitents move to either side of the priest to receive a gift from a minister, and then they return by the side aisles. The choir sings several songs during this time.

11

VII. Common Penance:

A priest asks the people to open their gifts to page 17 and to read aloud John 3:16 from their *Personal Bible*.

VIII. Concluding Song:

"Glory And Praise To Our God" by Dan Schutte, S.J.

Suggestions:

1. *Personal Bibles* may be purchased inexpensively from Little Bible Ministry — Saratoga, PA 19464.

2. If you do not purchase the *Personal Bible*, you could print your own card containing the passage from John 3:16.

3. We recommend a simple mobile with empty boxes, Christmas wrapped. We also recommend, if possible, that the gift of the miniature Bible or Scripture card be wrapped with Christmas paper.

4. The following appropriate songs may also be used for this service:
"Patience, people" by John Foley, S.J.
"Amazing Grace" & "Blest Be The Lord" by Dan Schutte, S.J.
"I Lift Up My Soul" by Tim Manion
"Peace Prayer" by John Foley, S.J.
"Awake, O Sleeper" by Balhoff, Ducote, Daigle
"Lift Up Your Hearts" by Roc O'Connor, S.J.

COMMUNAL RECONCILIATION SERVICE NUMBER 3

Theme: Wise Men and Women Still Seek Him — A Challenge to Change

Dominant Symbol: *Incense*

"We observed his star at its rising and have come to pay him homage." (Mt 2:2).

Theme: (To be printed on the order of service for silent reading by the congregation.)

Life, of its very nature, is a journey from birth to death. Also, knowingly or not, it's a search for God. Since the incarnation, the search is focused on Jesus. Like the Magi, we may seek Jesus in the wrong places — in the palaces and in the busy cities. Like the Magi, we may have to change our thinking in order to find Jesus in the quiet spots and in the most unlikely people and places. The challenge tonight is to awaken our hearts and minds to the Word of God so that, like the Magi, we will be led to the Savior in this sacrament of Reconciliation and to the Eucharist on Christmas.

I. Introduction:

(Three readers come out from the sacristy into the sanctuary, two women at the pulpit and a man at the stand on the side by the tabernacle. They give the following choral reading.)

ALL: Hustle and bustle; bustle and hustle.

READER 1: Christmas is always such a busy time, buying gifts.

READER 2: There is scarcely time even to go to church.

READER 3: There is scarcely time even to be by oneself, let alone to pray.

READER 1: Let us listen to all the voices of the hustle and bustle of Christmas . . . (Now various ads are played on the tape recorder. After the ads are finished, readers 2 and 3 (the women readers) begin each sentence and Reader 1 (the man) finishes them.)

READER 2 and 3: Hustle and bustle . . .

READER 1: And yet, we too can be wise men and wise women seeking Jesus in the depths of our hearts.

READER 2 and 3: Hustle and bustle . . .

READER 1: And yet we can praise and thank Him.

The readers exit and the entrance procession is readied. The ministers are assembled in the rear of the church. The lights are turned up in the sanctuary. The procession lines up as follows: Two liturgical dancers come up with incensors: two servers carry up candles and ten

13

servers bring up the lit incense sticks; then comes the lector with a lectionary or Bible and finally the two priests. One cantor, then two cantors, the song leader, then the choir and finally the congregation sing, "O Come, O Come Emmanuel" as the procession moves down the aisle. Those carrying candles place them in the sanctuary; the liturgical dancers stand beside the priests' chairs and the servers place the incense sticks into play putty in the candle holders. The priests walk up directly to the chairs.

II. Opening Prayer

"Lord, you invite us tonight to come as a community of faith to adore You and thank You for the gift of forgiveness. Like the Magi, we bring our lowly gifts of praise and adoration to You as You reveal your priceless gift of forgiveness. Amen."

III. Liturgy of the Word:

A. First Reading: Isaiah 60:4-6 (The prophecy of the coming of the Wise Men).

B. Sing: "Seek the Lord" by Roc O'Connor, S.J. (refrain only) (The liturgical dancers dance to this song and conclude by kneeling on the top step. Then the priest who will proclaim the Gospel, picks up the Bible from the manger and processes to the pulpit, with the liturgical dancers leading the way and standing at either side of the pulpit. After the song, the liturgical dancers process out the side sacristy exit with the censors.)

C. Gospel: Matthew 2:1-12 (*Stand*) (The Magi seek the Child Jesus)

C. Homily Hints:

1. Life — a journey, a seeking for God; we're all on pilgrimage.

   ● "Our hearts are restless till they rest in Thee." (Augustine)

   ● Wise Men represent a new kind of search: 1) Not the infinite spiritual being, like Yahweh 2) Rather a God incarnated in a tiny child called Jesus.

2. Wise Men used all the natural tools to find Jesus — astrology, the science of their day, but were ultimately helpless to find the savior — they had to go to the Scriptures of the Jews.

3. Purpose of the trip of the Wise men:

   ● To give Jesus homage and worship.

   ● To present Him gifts — but also to receive the gift of salvation — Magi represent Gentiles or all of us.

4. Jesus, on the other hand, demanded a change in the Magi:

   ● They no longer sought Him in palaces and kingly array. They humbled themselves by going to a stable.

14

● They risked — disobeying Herod and obeyed a vision or a dream.

5. What's all that got to do with us and Advent and reconciliation?

● Wise men and women still seek Him — although Jesus came to earth 2000 years ago, each generation must discover Him anew.

● How do people discover Jesus today? 1) Desire in heart leading to a journey, a search. 2) Searching the Scriptures as they are explained by the church. That's why we put the Scriptures in the manger.

● What is the purpose of our trip? 1) Give homage and worship 2) Present gifts of frankincense of praise 3) But also to receive gifts from Jesus — reconciliation and salvation — what we're all about tonight.

● Just as Magi found Jesus in Bethlehem, The House of Bread, we find Jesus in the bread of the House of God — Christmas Eucharist.

● What detours us in our journey? 1) Being duped by riches or plain old commercialism 2) Lack of perseverance — we can grow weary or indifferent or lazy 3) Can lose our faith — believe that the trip is an illusion 4) Can become too busy — seek Christmas in hustle and bustle of a city like Jerusalem 5) Can seek Him among high and mighty powers.

6. Tonight we want to get beyond tinsel and little baby and gifts to the idea of thanks, praise and homage. That's why we give you a *special* symbol tonight of incense — our basic symbol. We ask you to take this home and on Christmas burn incense and then say the short prayer in homage of the Savior — the healing Savior who forgives tonight. (see suggestion two)

IV. Examination of Conscience:

(The examination of conscience tonight is reflective imagining. The presider will lead you in this process.)

PRESIDER: "Tonight, for the examination of conscience, Jesus invites you to look inside yourself as He beckons you along the path to forgiveness. Visualize your internal journey towards Christ, the Savior. Please close your eyes and let your hands relax and now the muscles of your face, allowing the tensions to flow out of your body. Listen to the deepening silence in the church. Now let your imagination run loose. Imagine yourself in a beautiful forest on a summer day. The sun is beginning to warm your skin. Before you is a path in the woods. You begin up the path and notice it is familiar because you have walked along this path of forgiveness before. As you walk into the forest, you see the first sidepath. It is marked "*Laziness*" and it leads to a beautiful clearance in the forest where you see many ham-

15

mocks. Down that path are broken promises and broken commitments. Down that path is *"Negligence"* in praying and going to church. That sidepath briefly seems attractive but you decide to continue up the main path. You walk further and again you notice a sidepath. It is marked *"Selfish Pleasure."* Maybe you have gone down that path too, whether it's overindulgence in food or drink or irresponsible sex. You may still feel drawn by that path, but you shake your head and go resolutely forward. Suddenly, around a bend in the main path, you come across another sidepath named *"Riches."* This path is paved with gold and down the path lies cheating and deceit and compromise, trying to keep up with the Joneses. You hesitate but decide to go on. Suddenly, you come not to another sidepath, but to a separation into two paths. The path to your left is marked *"Pride and Complacency."* You feel you have been down that road before and it's a blind alley. It's a path that denies your sinfulness or a need for God. You decide you will never go down that alley again and you continue on the path to your right. Just before a hill, another sidepath leaves the main path as though it was your last detour, if you chose to go on it. It is marked *"Anger and Hatred."* Down that path lay bitterness and harsh words and revenge. You decide to avoid that detour and you climb the hill. The sun is shining brightly on a house that is marked "Bethlehem," which means "House of Bread." There Jesus is waiting. He looks on you with mercy, ready to forgive. He smiles kindly at you and suddenly, in his radiant light, you realize your sinfulness — the times you have strayed from the path and been disobedient to his Word; or been selfish or hateful or lazy or negligent. You see your sinfulness, and you are prepared once more to receive the Savior's healing touch, the gift of forgiveness.

V. Song:
"Lay Your Hands" by Carey Landry

VI. Sign of Sorrow: (*Kneel and make an act of sorrow together*)
"Lord, to the wise man and woman, all is gift and all gifts should lead to You, the Giver. It's only the abuse of your gifts that become the sidepaths leading away from You. We come with humility to confess to You and to the whole church that we have sinned by abusing your gifts. We ask for wisdom, healing and forgiveness. We beg You this night to give us the courage to begin anew, to change our lives and follow You. Amen."

Sing: "Day by Day" by Stephen Schwartz (from *Godspell*)

VII. Receiving the Symbol of Reconciliation and Absolution
A. We ask each person to follow the ushers up to the front step of the middle aisle. Each penitent approaches one of the priests and to his question: "Will you receive Christ's healing touch?" answers: "I will." The penitent then confesses and receives absolution. In the case

of non-sacramental penitential celebration, the priest imposes hands on the penitent.

B. After the absolution or the laying on of hands, the penitent goes to a minister on either side to receive a box of incense, a symbolic gift, before returning to the pew by way of the side aisle.

VIII. Sign of Peace: (*Stand*)
Sing: "The Peace of the Lord" by Gary Ault

IX. Common Penance:
The cantor will lead a song in litany of thanks and the congregation should follow the lead of the choir in singing the response after each phrase of the litany.

> LEADER: For the gift of the Spirit, wind and fire . . .
> ALL: Jesus, Jesus, thanks and praise.
> LEADER: For the gift of saving death . . .
> ALL: Jesus, Jesus, thanks and praise.
> LEADER: For the gift of your body and blood . . .
> ALL: Jesus, Jesus, thanks and praise.
> LEADER: For the gift of your healing forgiveness . . .
> ALL: Jesus, Jesus, thanks and praise.
> LEADER: For the gift of life, now and hereafter . . .
> ALL: Jesus, Jesus, thanks and praise.
> LEADER: For the gift of the church, our brothers and sisters . . .
> ALL: Jesus, Jesus, thanks and praise.
> LEADER: For the gift of your child-like faith . . .
> ALL: Jesus, Jesus, thanks and praise.
> LEADER: For the gift of hope as you conquered death . . .
> ALL: Jesus, Jesus, thanks and praise.
> LEADER: For the gift of love that mirrors your own . . .
> ALL: Jesus, Jesus, thanks and praise.
> LEADER: For the gift of family, its warmth and its love . . .
> ALL: Jesus, Jesus, thanks and praise.
> LEADER: For the gift of friends more precious than gold . . .
> ALL: Jesus, Jesus, thanks and praise.
> LEADER: For the gift of creation, the work of your hands . . .
> ALL: Jesus, Jesus, thanks and praise.

X. Concluding Song:
"Turn to Me" by John Foley, S.J.

Suggestions:
1. In the Holy Family Reconciliation Service, small golden boxes and incense sticks were purchased inexpensively. We included a prayer to be said when the incense was lit on Christmas day.

2. A simple way of giving a gift to people would be to give them an incense stick taped on a plain card with the following prayer. "Father we thank You for the priceless gift of forgiveness through Jesus, our savior. May our prayer of praise, like incense, rise up before You. Amen."

3. The following appropriate songs could be used:
"Awake, O Sleeper" by Balhoff, Ducote, Daigle
"For Everything There is a Time" by Donald Reagan
"I Long For You" by Balhoff, Ducote, Daigle
"Light of the World" by Tom Kendzia

Part II
Lent

COMMUNAL RECONCILIATION SERVICE NUMBER 4

Theme: Invitation To New Life

Dominant Symbol: *Sacramental symbols, especially water, oil, stole.*
"I came that they might have Life and have it to the full." (Jn. 10:10)
(The lights in the church are lowered. The priest celebrants enter directly from the sacristy and go to their seats. The congregation remains seated also. Then after a few moments of silence, the lector announces the theme.)

I. Introduction:

A. The Theme: "Among all the channels of grace, there are seven special channels designated by the church, called the sacraments. Today we want to highlight three sacraments — Baptism, Confirmation, and Reconciliation. These sacraments invite us to New Life.

B. Entrance Procession: In a semi-darkened church, background music begins. Then three lay ministers dressed in choir robes lead three other lay ministers, dressed similarly. Down the right aisle, one candle bearer leads a minister bearing a bowl of water as a symbol of Baptism. Down the left aisle, another candle bearer leads a minister bearing a flask of oil, the symbol of Confirmation: finally down the center aisle another candle-bearer leads a minister bearing a stole, the symbol of Reconciliation. The candle-bearers place their candles on stands near the symbols and the other ministers place the symbols in their proper positions in the sanctuary (c.f. diagram). The symbols are displayed in the following fashion from left to right:

Baptism — bowl of water
Confirmation — jar of oil
Matrimony — wedding candle
Holy Eucharist — loaf of bread and grapes
Holy Orders — chalice
Anointing of Sick — sick call set
Reconciliation — stole

C. Opening Prayer: (*Priest stands and asks congregation to do likewise.*) "Lord you came to give life, life in its fullness. It was from the cross that the life of the Spirit and all sacramental life follows. Lord, through your cross, may you heal, forgive, and bring New Life. We ask this through Christ, our Savior. Amen."

D. The priest will incense the symbols displayed before the altar, and then be seated.

II. Liturgy of the Word: (*Congregation sits*)

A. Romans 6:1-4: (We are called to die to sin with Christ so as to rise with Him to New Life.)

B. Response: Remember your love and your faithfulness, O Lord, remember your people, and have mercy on us, Lord. "Remember Your Love" by Ducote, Daigle

C. John 19:33-35: (Stand) (Soldiers pierced Jesus' side as He was dying on the cross. From his side came forth water and blood, the symbols of Baptism and Eucharist.)

D. Homily Hints:
It would be good to explain briefly the symbol-displays of the seven sacraments.

1. The cross is the source of all sacramental life.

2. By Baptism and Confirmation especially, we are all called to be disciples of Christ. By our sinfulness we fail to follow Jesus in his Way of the Cross and in turn become anti-life.

3. Through the Sacrament of Reconciliation, we can heal the cancer that is sin and restore the brokenness of our relationship to Christ and to our brothers and sisters.

4. Although Baptism is initiation into the "Christ-Life," Reconciliation has often been called a "Second Baptism."

5. Through the Sacrament of Reconciliation, we renew the call to our discipleship initiated in Baptism and accept our adult commitment of Confirmation.

E. Song: "Turn To Me: by John Foley, S.J.

III. Examination of Conscience: (*Remain Seated*)

LEADER: For the times I have wandered away from my Father's House like the Prodigal Son . . . (pause)

ALL: Lord, help me say "Yes" to New Life

LEADER: For the times I have been ashamed to call myself a Christian . . . (pause)

ALL: Lord, help me say "Yes" to New Life

LEADER: For the times I never got involved with the church and its mission . . . (pause)

ALL: Lord, help me say "Yes" to New Life

LEADER: For the times I neglected the sacrament of Reconciliation and its call for forgiveness . . . (pause)

ALL: Lord, help me say "Yes" to New Life

LEADER: For the times I've failed to live up to my vocational commitment, whether as a religious, married, or single person . . . (pause)

ALL: Lord, help me say "Yes" to New Life

LEADER: For the times out of selfishness or hardness of heart I have not admitted my sinfulness . . . (pause)

ALL: Lord, help me say "Yes" to New Life

LEADER: For the times I have squandered the Father's Gifts, whether of time, talents or material possessions . . . (pause)

ALL: Lord, help me say "Yes" to New Life

LEADER: For the times I have separated myself from the members of God's Family, through hatred, pride, stubbornness, slander . . . (pause)

ALL: Lord, help me say "Yes" to New Life

LEADER: For the times I have been slow to say "I'm sorry," or seek forgiveness of others and of God . . . (pause)

ALL: Lord, help me say "Yes" to New Life

LEADER: For the times I've failed my faith community by not joining in Sunday worship when I might easily have done so . . . (pause)

ALL: Lord, help me say "Yes" to New Life

IV. Sign of Sorrow:

As an act of sorrow, the priest and people kneel and recite together the Confiteor: "We confess to almighty God, and to you, our brothers and sisters, that we have sinned through our own fault (we strike our breasts) in our thoughts and in our words, in what we have done, and in what we have failed to do; and we ask blessed Mary, ever virgin, all the angels and saints, to pray for us to the Lord our God."

V. Receiving of the Symbol and Absolution:

Ask congregation to sit until ushers direct them, pew by pew, to approach the altar. The people are asked to come up and follow the ushers' directions as they form two lines in the center aisle. Near the front pew of the center aisle, two lay ministers hold bowls of water. First, each penitent takes holy water and makes the sign of the cross as a symbol of the cleansing water of Baptism. Secondly, the penitent approaches the priest to receive the blessing of oil on his/her forehead. During the absolution the priest places the stole on his/her shoulder as a symbol of forgiveness of sins. (When using the non-sacramental penitential celebration, the priest places the stole on the penitent's shoulder and anoints with oil while asking the question, "Will you

answer the call to New Life?'' To which the person responds, "Yes."
The penitent then returns to his/her pew.)

VI. Common Penance:

People stand and sing the "Our Father."

VII. Sign of Peace: "Peace Prayer" by John Foley, S.J.

Suggestions:

1. Instead of the elaborate decor as described in Suggestion two, a less elaborate decor could be used. With the cross always as the source of the sacramental signs, three sacraments (Baptism, Confirmation and Reconciliation) could be highlighted instead of all seven.

2. Liturgical Setting: Darkened church, spotlight on large wooden cross in center of sanctuary. Rainbow colors of cloth emanate from the cross. At the end of each piece of cloth, one of the sacramental symbols is placed. Since three sacraments are being highlighted, these three symbols are strategically placed in the sanctuary arrangement.

3. Other suggested songs for this service:
"If God Is For Us" by John Foley, S.J.
"You Are Near" by Dan Schutte, S.J.
"I Long for You" by Balhoff, Ducot, Daigle
"Light of the World" by Tom Kendzia
"Redeemer Lord" by John Foley, S.J.

COMMUNAL RECONCILIATION SERVICE NUMBER 5

Theme: Were You There?

Dominant Symbol: *Decal of Cross*

"He was pierced for our offenses, crushed for our sins." (Is. 53:5)

Introduction:

(The present introduction was placed in the order of service to be read silently by the congregation before the service began.)

We have a tendency to look at others as being responsible for the crucifixion of an innocent man like Jesus. We salve our consciences by saying, "Had I been there I would never have participated in his betrayal, judgment and crucifixion." Yet, Isaiah says, "He was pierced for our offenses, crushed for our sins." Indeed we were there by reason of our sinfulness and we may even see part of ourselves in the characters who were physically present at the Good Friday crucifixion.

I. Liturgy of the Word: *(Remain seated)*

A. The priests enter in from the sanctuary. When they are seated, the lector comes to the pulpit as the choir sings the first verse of "Were You There?"

B. The lector gives a general introduction and in turn introduces the seven scripture characters who, in monologue-fashion, will share their thoughts. The characters in order of appearance are: 1) Judas, 2) Caiphas, 3) Woman from the mob, 4) Pilate, 5) Herod, 6) Barabbas, 7) Mary Magdalene

LECTOR: In the Gospels, many people are directly involved in the death of Jesus — the priests, the Pharisees, the Romans, the screaming mob. Some individuals we even know by name — Judas, Herod, Caiphas, Pilate. But in one sense, we are all responsible for the death of Jesus. Luke says in his Gospel: "It was now around midday, and darkness came over the whole land until mid-afternoon with an eclipse of the sun." (Lk. 23:44) Darkness. Darkness. Was it just evil men who destroyed Jesus or was it the evil in all of us, the darkness in all of us that killed Christ on Good Friday? Sometimes we wish the Gospel writers had better decribed the inner thoughts of the characters involved in the drama of the crucifixion of Jesus. We invite you to listen to the secret thoughts of characters like Pilate and Judas in order to see ourselves in their selfish ambition or skepticism or cruelty or sensual weakness. We ask you to identify with the characters so that we, too, might ask ourselves the question, "Were you there?" (Reads Luke 22:3-6)

24

JUDAS: I, Judas, was there. Had I known they would have killed Jesus, I wouldn't have turned him over to them. But was it really a *betrayal*? At one time I put my full trust in Jesus. But He was not the Messiah I thought he was; yes, I became disillusioned. When Jesus spoke of freedom, it was not from Rome. Instead of destroying the cruel yoke of Rome (Jesus had special power — I saw it work.), He talked about turning the other cheek. Instead of promising riches, He asked people to sell what they had and give it to the poor. And when I tried to stop a woman, in some foolish show of affection, from wasting expensive perfume, he publicly rebuked me. Yes, I became disillusioned and felt Jesus was a dreamer, a dangerous dreamer. I helped the authorities stop a deceiver of the people. I took the money but I really didn't want Him to die on the cross. Yes, I was there. Were you there too?

LECTOR: (Reads John 11:49-50)

CAIPHAS: I was there, in the background. As high priest, I, Caiphas, had to assume my responsibility and this Jesus was a dangerous man. Not only did He blaspheme and claim to be God, but He was a corrupter of the people. Generally, the Pharisees and I do not agree but in this we did. Besides breaking the Sabbath, He predicted the destruction of the temple and drove out money-changers on his own authority. And, after all, who was this Jesus but a country bumpkin, an unlettered carpenter's son who had the arrogance to challenge our teachers and scribes? Yes, I know this Jesus called us "proud" and uncharitable, but only the riff-raff, the mob, was deceived by him. But most of all, I had to protect the people. This so-called messiah, who had a gift of deceiving the people, could destroy the peace and bring the Roman hordes crashing down upon us. Yes, I was there because I needed to be there. Were you there?

LECTOR: (Reads John 19:14-15)

WOMAN FROM THE MOB: I was there, part of the crowd. You can't blame me. I believed what I was told and I did what I was told. I'm just an ordinary patriotic Jewish woman, and I was caught in the crowd. Although I had heard that this Jesus was a gentle man who went about healing and doing good, He must have done something terribly wrong, something sacrilegious. Otherwise, why would the priests and Pharisees scream for his death? And after all, can thousands of people be wrong? Had you been in the crowd, would you have acted any differently? I was there, just an ordinary citizen. How about you? Were you there in the crowd, too?

LECTOR: (Reads John 19:12-16)

PILATE: Yes, I am Pilate and indeed I was there. History will probably say I could have prevented the Nazarene's death. But put yourself in my position. These Jews were a god-awful nation of people — hardheaded, fanatical and contemptuous. There was never any pleasing them. Once, when I brought painted portraits of the Emperor into the Jewish temple, the Jews complained to the Emperor himself. Even Rome feared their fanaticism and did not back me when I took action against them. I had only one thought — advancement out of this uncivilized post. Then they brought this harmless Jesus to be tried in my court. He told me He was a son of God. I don't deny it — I am a superstitious man, and I don't like prosecuting gods, even Jewish ones. So I did my best to free Him. Instead the mob asked for a murderer, a certain Barabbas, to be set free. Well, if you were there, hearing them shout that if I set Him free, I wouldn't be the emperor's friend — well, another report to the emperor would have meant the end of my career. After all, a person must think of himself; you get ahead by playing the court game. Wouldn't you agree? Would you have done differently if you had been there?

LECTOR: (Reads Luke 23:7-9)

HEROD: Yes, I was there. This Jesus was a fool with his message of sacrifice and selflessness. What did it get him but the cross? After all, what is there in life except pleasure. Wouldn't you agree? Life is such a bore and pleasure is the only thing that gives life any meaning. But back to Jesus. I could have saved Him, this Jesus, if He had just amused me. Had He just pulled a few tricks, showed me some magic, who knows? I might have even . . . followed Him. But He turned out to be a fool who wouldn't even talk to me. Yes, I was there, and I saw Him hanging from a cross through my window. Perhaps you saw Him. Perhaps you were there, too.

LECTOR: (Reads Luke 23:14,16-19)

BARABBAS: Call me Barabbas or whatever name you wish. I was there and I saw this Jesus die. After all, anyone would be curious about someone who becomes a free ticket out of jail. I didn't understand the man. I understand hate: good, clean hate. Yes, I even killed Romans and plan to do it again until every Roman is driven from our land. But Jesus. He didn't curse them as they put a crown of thorns on his head and He stood there like a lamb as they spit on his face. Then He accepted the cross without a murmur like a man predestined to carry it. I guess I don't understand anyone who doesn't fight back. Yes, I was there on that Friday. Were you there?

LECTOR: (Reads John: 19:25-26)

MARY MAGDALENE: Yes, I, Mary Magdalene, was there. I saw the priests and Pharisees as they cruelly mocked Him. And I understood sin as I had never understood sin before. I understood their sin, I understood my sins. And in some mysterious way, I also understood what Jesus was doing. He was taking their sins, my sins and nailing them in his flesh to the cross. And as I looked into his eyes and upon his body wracked in pain, I could hear Him murmur, "Father, forgive them for they know not what they do." Yes, I understood what my sins were about and what God's love was about. I was there and I helped put Him on the cross through my past sins. Maybe you are without sin, but I know that I was there. Were you there?

C. Choir sings second verse of "Were You There?"

D. Priest reads Isaiah 53:4-6. (Israel as Suffering Servant)

E. Homily Hints:

1. If we see the trial/crucifixion/death of Jesus as purely historical, the answer to the question, "Were you there?", would be a resounding "NO." The death of Jesus is more than just a historical event. Paul says he died for all.

2. His death surpassed time and has universal significance.

3. In some way, the mystery of evil was at work at Calvary. It was more than just the evil of the Romans or the Jews — it was the evil of all humankind that caused the death of Jesus. See Romans 5:18-19.

4. Tonight we heard seven characters reveal their rationalizations for their role in the crucifixion while also clearly revealing their dominant weakness or sinfulness. At the same time they became a mirror of ourselves — Judas represents our own capacity for greed and betrayal; Pilate, our ambition which overrides principles; the sensuality of Mary Magdalene; the smugness of Caiphas; the excuse of following the crowd as seen in the woman from the mob; the hatred and hardness of Barabbas and the pampering self-centeredness of a Herod.

5. The dramatic moment of honesty for each of us in the face of the history and mystery of the crucifixion is to admit our guilt, our sinfulness and say, "Yes, we were there." We need not despair like Judas, but rather turn to the Lord like Mary Magdalene. As truly as *our sinfulness* was present 2000 years ago, so too was Christ's forgiveness present there. Christ's forgiveness is universal, applying to every age.

6. As a symbol of our forgiveness, we will be giving you a decal which includes a morning offering which reminds us every day of the forgiving death of Jesus. You can put it on your bathroom mirror, or in your kitchen, or in your car.

(After the homily, the lights are turned up and the congregation joins the choir in singing the third verse of "Were You There?")

II. Examination of Conscience: *(Kneel)*

One of the priests leads the Examination of Conscience. Pause before the response: "Lord, forgive me."

LEADER: Like Judas, I was there by my greed and skepticism . . . (pause)

ALL: Lord, forgive me.

LEADER: Like Pilate, I was there through my ambition and compromise of principle . . . (pause)

ALL: Lord, forgive me.

LEADER: Like Mary Magdalene, I was there by my sensuality . . . (pause)

ALL: Lord, forgive me.

LEADER: Like Caiphas, I was there by my pride and smugness . . . (pause)

ALL: Lord, forgive me.

LEADER: Like the woman from the mob, I was there by my human respect and herd instinct that didn't accept personal responsibility . . . (pause)

ALL: Lord, forgive me.

LEADER: Like Barabbas, I was there by my hatred and hardened heart . . . (pause)

ALL: Lord, forgive me.

LEADER: Like Herod, I was there by my self-centeredness and my shallowness . . . (pause)

ALL: Lord, forgive me.

(Pause for further private examination.)

ALL SING: "Turn to Me" by John Foley, S.J.

III. Sign of Sorrow: *(Kneel and read together)*

"Were you there? Yes, Lord, I was there, and for my sins I ask your pardon. As I begin a new day, I give You praise for your forgiving love. Amen."

IV. Receiving of the Symbol of Absolution:

A. First, the penitent approaches the priest and the priest asks, "Were you there?" The penitent replies, "I was." Then the priest gives absolution or, if the non-sacramental penitential celebration is used, the priest imposes hands on the penitent.

B. The penitent goes to the minister on either side to receive the decal of the cross.

V. Sign of Peace:

"Peace Is Flowing Like a River" by Carey Landry

VI. Common Penance:

Make a resolution to attend at least one of the Holy Week liturgies — Holy Thursday, Good Friday, or Holy Satuday.

VII. Concluding Song:

"Glory and Praise To Our God" by Dan Shutte, S.J.

Suggestions:

1. The monologue may be presented in a very simple manner or an increasingly elaborate style, which could include memorization, costuming, simple props, and appropriate lighting.

2. The cross decals may be reproduced inexpensively or a very simple cross and prayer may be mimeographed. The following is a sample: "Yes, Lord, I was there, and for my sins, I ask your pardon. As I begin a new day, I give you praise for your forgiving love. Amen."

3. The following appropriate songs could be used:
"Deep River" (Negro spiritual)
"Poor Homeless Stranger" (Negro spiritual)

COMMUNAL RECONCILIATION SERVICE NUMBER 6

Theme: The Passover Lamb Saves Us

Dominant Symbol: *Passover Prayer Card*

"You were delivered . . . by Christ's blood . . . the blood of the spotless, unblemished lamb . . . " (1 Pt 1:18-19).

Theme: (Read before the service begins)

The most important feast of the Jews is the Passover. It celebrated the liberation of the Jews from the slavery in Egypt. When Moses asked Pharoah to let his people go, Pharoah refused. Then Yahweh sent plagues, and in the final plague, an angel of death killed the eldest son of each Egyptian family. The Jewish families were spared by following God's instructions of putting the blood of a lamb on the lintel and the doorposts of their homes. Down through the centuries, the Passover ritual celebrated the liberation of the Jews from Egypt and a lamb was still eaten and its blood placed over the doorway. At the Last supper, Jesus not only celebrated the Jewish Passover, but He also instituted the Christian Passover. Through Jesus' death and resurrection, Christians are liberated from sin and death. At the Last Supper, Jesus did not use a lamb's blood to save us, but actually became the Lamb of God, whose very blood liberates us from the slavery of Satan and from death's power over us.

I. Introduction (*Remain seated*)

A. The lights are dimmed to highlight the wooden cross placed on the altar. After the reading of the theme, the cantor will intone "Agnus Dei." Then the song leader leads the people in the first verse of "Lamb of God, who takes away the sins of the world, have mercy on us." While the first verse is being sung, an acolyte brings a vigil light down the side aisle and places it on the altar. There is a brief pause and a second acolyte brings a vigil light down the side aisle for verse two. Finally there is a pause. During the singing of the third verse, the priests come down the center aisle following the third acolyte who carries a vigil light. The lector carries the Scripture to a stand and an acolyte carries an image of the Lamb of God. When the priests get to the sanctuary, they bow — one goes to the cross to put the image of the lamb upon the cross, and one goes to the chairs. After both priests are at the chairs, an opening prayer is said.

B. Opening Prayer: (*Stand*)

"Lord, we are gathered tonight as people of God to be reminded of our need for liberation — to be freed of sin. We know that Jesus remains our Savior, the Lamb of God who died for our sins. As we listen to Your Holy Word, O Lord, touch our hearts, burdened with sin and liberate us again from sin and death. Amen."

II. Liturgy of the Word: (*Be seated*)

Introduction: A lector goes to remove the Bible from its stand and awaits the priest who will incense the Book.

A. First reading is from Exodus: "Then the LORD told Moses, "One more plague will I bring upon Pharoah and upon Egypt. After that he will let you depart. In fact, he will not merely let you go; he will drive you away. Moses then said, "Thus says the LORD: At midnight I will go forth through Egypt. Every first-born in this land shall die, from the first-born of Pharoah on the throne to the first-born of the slave-girl at the handmill, as well as all the first-born of the animals. But among the Israelites and their animals not even a dog shall growl, so that you may know how the LORD distinguishes between the Egyptians and the Israelites." (Ex. 11:1,4,5,7) It is because of this intervention of the Lord that Moses commands Israel to celebrate the Passover. We read in the Book of Exodus the following words: "Moses called all the elders of Israel and said to them, 'Go and procure lambs for your families, and slaughter them as Passover victims.' (Ex. 12:21) "The lamb must be a year-old male and without blemish. You may take it from either the sheep or the goats. You shall keep it until the fourteenth day of this month, and then, with the whole assembly of Israel present, it shall be slaughtered during the evening twilight." (Ex. 12:5-6) "Then take a bunch of hyssop, and dipping it in the blood that is in the basin, sprinkle the lintel and the two doorposts with this blood. Seeing the blood . . . the LORD will pass over that door and not let the destroyer come into your houses to strike you down. (Ex. 12:22-23) It is the passover of the LORD. For on this same night I will go through Egypt . . . I, the LORD! But the blood will mark the houses where you are. Seeing the blood, I will pass over you; thus, when I strike the land of Egypt, no destructive blow will come upon you." (Ex. 12:11-13.) This is the word of the Lord.

B. Response: "Worthy Is the Lamb" by Bob Dufford, SJ. (Refrain only — twice.)

C. Second Reading: 1 Peter 1: 18-21 (We have been redeemed by the blood of Christ.) (*Please stand.*) "Glory and Praise to You, Lord Jesus Christ."

D. Gospel: John 19:31-35 (Jesus, the Passover Lamb, dies for us.)

E. Homily Hints:

1. We are accustomed to hearing the phrase, "The Lamb of God,"

in Mass, especially before communion ("Behold the Lamb of God").
What does it mean?

2. What does the "lamb" mean in Scripture?

● In the Old Testament — the ritual of the Passover and
its biblical background — the ritual of the scapegoat on the
feast of the Atonement and its meaning.

● The meaning of the Passover in the New Testament,
St. John's Gospel — Jesus became 'The Lamb of God" —
the Passover Lamb.

3. Comparison of "being" saved by the Passover Lamb in the Old
Testament and "Lamb of God" in the New Testament.

● In the Old Testament: "Passover Lamb" symbol of
freedom from slavery by Egyptians and salvation from the
Angel of Death.

● In New Testament: Jesus, Lamb of God, frees us from
the slavery of Satan and from death.

4. Meaning of the cards we gave to you tonight: The cards have
two sides:

● One side is red and represents the Lamb slain for our
sins: We ask you to place it on the lintel of your door as a
symbol of salvation from sin and death.

● The other side is gold and represents the victorious
Lamb of Revelation. On Easter turn the card around to
represent "victory" through Jesus, our Paschal Lamb.

5. At the sign of peace, we ask you to do something special: that
you place a sign of the cross on the forehead of your neighbor as a
reminder of Baptism and liberation by the Passover Lamb.

6. Finally, look at the image of the Lamb on the cross in the sanctuary. From the side of Jesus (according to John's Gospel) flows water
and blood, the symbols of Baptism and our Eucharist. We prepare for
our Easter Eucharistic celebration: liberation from sin and death.

Song: "Were You There?" (Negro spiritual)

III. Examination of Conscience: (*Remain seated*)
Introduction: "Lord, by your death on the cross, You bore the sins of
the past, present and future. As the Lamb of God You bore the pride
of the Pharisees, the betrayal of Judas, the cowardice of Pilate. But
You also bear the sins of our generation and all future generations."

(Follow the directions of the leader for the Examination of Conscience.)

LEADER: Lamb of God, you who bear our sins of violence and hatred . . . (Pause)

ALL: Have mercy on us.

LEADER: Lamb of God, you who bear betrayal by us, your closest friends . . . (pause)

ALL: Have mercy on us.

LEADER: Lamb of God, you who bear our cowardice and sins of human respect . . . (pause)

ALL: Have mercy on us.

LEADER: Lamb of God, you who bear our sins of conformity and ignorance . . . (pause)

ALL: Have mercy on us.

LEADER: Lamb of God, you who bear our sins of pride and ridicule . . . (pause)

ALL: Have mercy on us.

LEADER: Lamb of God, you who bear our sins of lying, slander and injustice . . . (pause)

ALL: Have mercy on us.

LEADER: Lamb of God, you who bear our sins of soft living and selfish pleasure . . . (pause)

ALL: Have mercy on us. (Pause and search your own heart for your sins which may have burdened Jesus, the Lamb of God.)

IV. Sign of Sorrow: (*Kneel*)

"Lord, Jesus Christ, You are the Lamb of God, You take away the sins of the World. Through the grace of the Holy Spirit, strengthen my friendship with Your Father, cleanse me from every stain of sin in the blood You shed for me. Raise me to new life for the glory of your name."

V. Symbolic Action of Reconciliation and Absolution

(Be seated until it's time for you to come forward. The choir will sing during this time)

A. First the penitent approaches the priest and the priest gives absolution, or, if it is a non-sacramental penitential celebration, the priest places his hands on the penitent's head.

B. At the same time, the priest asks the question: "Does the blood of Jesus set you free?" The penitent responds, "Yes."

C. Finally, the penitent goes to a minister for a prayer card and returns to the pew.

VI. Sign of Peace: *(Please stand)*

The congregation makes a sign of the cross on his or her neighbor's forehead to remind us of Baptism (which set us free) and of our participation in redemption. We also help set people free. The congregation waits for the presider to give the sign of the cross to the people in the center aisle. The congregation, in turn, gives the sign to their nearest neighbor all the way to those in the side aisle. As they give the sign, they say, "Peace be with you."

Song: "Peace is Flowing Like a River" by Carey Landry

VII. Common Penance:

As a penance, you are requested to attend one or more of the Holy Week services.

VIII. Concluding Song:

"Praise the Lord, My Soul" by John Foley, S.J.

Suggestions:

1. In the Holy Family Reconciliation Service, we used a plain, large wooden cross. One of the parishioners drew a lamb (which symbolically showed the blood going into a chalice) and the ministers carried the

symbol up in procession to place on the cross. The lamb was made of white styrofoam and simply painted. If this presents difficulties, a lamb could be placed on the cross before the service begins.

2. Our Passover Card had two sides: a) one side showed the lamb with the blood pouring into the chalice with a quote of 1 Peter 1: 18-19. We had a red cross on that side. This was to be hung over the doorway until Easter. b) The other side had a triumphant lamb with a paschal banner and a quote from Revelation 7: 16-17. We had a gold cross on this side. This side of the card was to be turned for the Easter season. Simpler versions of the same could be used.

3. The following appropriate songs could be used:
"Jesus The Lord" by Roc O'Connor, S.J.
"May We Praise You" by John Foley S.J.
"Only This I Want" by Dan Schutte, S.J.
"All I Ask Of You" by Gregory Norbet, O.S.B.
"Amazing Grace" (Traditional)
"Dwelling Place" by John Foley, S.J.

COMMUNAL RECONCILIATION SERVICE NUMBER 7

Theme: Redemption In The Blood of Christ

Dominant Symbol: *The Nail*

"You are delivered . . . by Christ's blood beyond all price . . ." (Pt. 1:18-19)

I. Introduction:

A. The theme is announced by the lector: "In being nailed to the cross, Christ paid a great price that we might be liberated from sin. He continues to liberate us today if we but accept his forgiveness and his healing grace. Our world today is enmeshed in its own kinds of sins of violence, greed and ishonesty. Let us now listen to the catalogue of sins we hear in our daily *bad news*."

B. Beginning of the Service:
1. The priests and servers are lined up at the rear of the church with two candles and incense.
2. The large wooden cross is in the middle of the sanctuary, covered with newspaper clippings of violence, etc. The lights in the church are turned off and the spotlight goes on the cross.
3. As the international news (war and violence and threat of nuclear proliferation, etc.) is read, the priests in procession move one third of the way down the aisle. The news lasts 20-30 seconds and then the refrain from the song is sung (or played on record).
"My People" by Bob Dufford, S.J.
Then after that, the national news is given (senseless killings, libel suits, etc.) and the procession moves towards the front of the church. Again the refrain, "My People." Finally, there's local news and some bad news and a final time for the refrain, "My People." (Recordings of international, national and local news are made from the local radio or T.V. station.)
4. The priests will stop three times before ending up at the cross, which is then incensed.

C. Opening Prayer:
"Lord, when You were nailed to the cross, the world came to know the depth, the length and breadth of your love. We gaze upon your cross as the sign of reconciliation for the world and as the sign of our personal forgiveness, no matter what our sins may be. We contemplate the

nails symbolic of the cost, as a sign of the price You paid that we might be freed from sin and healed by your forgiveness. Lord, You are the crucified Savior whom we need yesterday, today and forever. Amen."

D. The lector now comes forward with the Bible and there is an incensing of the Word of God.

II. Liturgy of the Word:

A. 1 Peter 1:17-21 (*Sit.*) (We are ransomed, not by money, but by Jesus' very own life.)

B. Response: Sing "Were You There?" (Negro Spiritual)

C. John 19:31-34: (*Stand*). (The source of all salvation and all sacramental life comes from Jesus Christ's death on the Cross.)

D. Homily Hints:

1. We've become accustomed to the cross and forget what a symbol of torture it was in Roman times. The instrument was borrowed from the Persians as a symbol of inhuman means of torture. So horrible was it that Roman citizens were exempt from it. It was reserved for criminals and runaway slaves. In those days, the freedom of slaves could be purchased if there was sufficient money. In this case Jesus became "The Slave" burdened with sin to free us, the slaves of sin.

2. In John's reading we are reminded that Jesus' forgiveness and mercy are enfleshed in the church's sacramental life down through the centuries. Water from Jesus' side becomes the symbol of Baptism which is the first sacrament of forgiveness. Blood from his wound represents the sacrifice on the cross which is renewed bloodlessly in the eucharistic celebration.

3. Our sacrament of reconciliation was called by the early Church Fathers "the second baptism" because it again cleaned us from sin.

4. Christ by shedding his blood has redeemed all people and has freed us from slavery and sin. This redemption needs to be applied to and accepted by each generation. All of us gathered here tonight are asked to repent in our hearts and to seek forgiveness in this sacrament.

5. After the priest gives absolution, the penitent is given a large nail (or a card with a nail on it) as a sign of his/her participation in the crucifixion of Jesus. For by our sins we too were there when they nailed Him to a tree.

III. Examination of Conscience: (*Sit*)

LEADER: Lord, we have sinned with our bodies, we have at times been lazy, sensuous, allowing our bodies to be masters of our spirits. For that You paid the price and were scourged mercilessly by soldiers . . . (pause)

ALL: Lord, heal our wounds.

LEADER: Lord, we have sinned in our thoughts, in our hearts and our imaginations. We have planned revenge, harbored grudges, made judgments about people, made evil plans. For that You paid the price with a crown of thorns . . . (pause)

ALL: Lord, heal our wounds.

LEADER: Lord, we have at times cheated, stolen and made money our god. For that, Lord, you paid the price and felt the blistering kiss of betrayal by a friend who sold You for thirty silver pieces . . . (pause)

ALL: Lord, heal our wounds.

LEADER: Lord, we have used our hands to form fists, to shut others out of our lives, to clutch in greed what we have. For that You paid the price and had nails driven into your hands . . . (pause)

ALL: Lord, heal our wounds.

LEADER: Lord, we have used our feet to walk away from good deeds or to walk knowingly into temptation. For that You paid the price by having nails driven into your feet . . . (pause)

ALL: Lord, heal our wounds.

IV. Sign of Sorrow: *(Kneel)*

As an act of sorrow, we are asked to cross our hands over our chests and recite together, following the lead of the priests, "Lamb of God, who takes away the sins of the world, have mercy on us. Lamb of God who takes away the sins of the world, have mercy on us. Lamb of God who takes away the sins of the world, grant us peace."

V. Receiving the Symbols of Reconciliation and Absolution:

We ask the people to follow the ushers' direction by coming down the center in two lines. Each person receives individual absolution and then steps to the side and is given a nail. During this time, the choir sings several songs. In case a non-sacramental penitential celebration is used, the priest places his hands on the head of each penitent for a second and the penitent then receives the symbol.

VI. Common Penance: *(Prayer before a crucifix — kneel and recite together)*

"Look down upon me, good and gentle Jesus, while before your face I humbly kneel and with burning soul, pray and beseech You to fix deep in my heart lively sentiments of faith, hope and charity; true contrition of my sins and a firm purpose of amendment. While I contemplate with great love and tender pity, your five most precious wounds, pondering over them within me, and calling to mind the words which David, your prophet, said to You, My Jesus: 'They have pierced my hands and my feet, they have numbered all my bones.' Amen."

VII. Sign of Peace

VIII. Concluding Song:

"Glory and Praise to Our God" by Dan Schutte, S.J.

Suggestions:

1. Newspaper articles and pictures can be taped to a wooden cross. The homilist might refer to the meaning of the newspaper articles which reflect the social sins of our day.

2. The nail that is used as a symbol for this service should be rather large. It could be distributed in many ways: as people enter church, or after they receive absolution. We recommend that it be attached to a card upon which a scriptural text is printed: "They crucified Him and the criminals as well, one on his right, and the other on his left." (Lk. 23:33)

3. The following songs would also be appropriate for this service:
"Jesus the Lord" by Roc O'Connor, S.J.
"May We Praise You" by John Foley, S.J.
"Save Us, O Lord" by Bob Dufford, S.J.
"All I Ask Of You" by Gregory Norbet, O.S.B. (Weston Priory)
"Amazing Grace" (Traditional)
"Dwelling Place" by John Foley, S.J.

COMMUNAL RECONCILIATION SERVICE NUMBER 8

Theme: By the Cross of Jesus We Are Saved

Dominant Symbol: *The Cross*

"If we have died with Christ, we believe we are also to live with him." (Rom. 6:8)

Theme: (To be read by a lector or priest.)

"To the world the cross seems like a cruel joke or an absurdity, but to the Christian, the cross is wisdom and its power is forgiveness and salvation. Jesus on the cross not only died for humankind in general but for each of us."

I. Introduction:

A. The lights are darkened in the church except for the sanctuary. A priest or assistants carry a large wooden cross down the center aisle and place it in a stand in a prominent place in the sanctuary. The congregation sings the following song while the procession is marching down the aisle. (Two acolytes could also carry candles.) Song: "Amazing Grace" (Traditional).

B. Opening Prayer: "Heavenly Father, lead us away from the wisdom of the world to the wisdom of the believers, the wisdom of the cross. Help us to find forgiveness in the power of your cross as we humbly beg for reconciliation with You and the church. We ask this through Christ, our Lord, and Savior. Amen."

II. Liturgy of the Word:

A. 1 Corinthians 1:18-25: (The cross is the wisdom of God.)

B. Response: Sing or recite: "Lord, by Your cross and resurrection, You have set us free. You are the Savior of the World."

C. Gospel: Mark 15: 33-39 (Clearly Jesus is truly the Son of Man.)

D. Homily Hints:

1. In the first reading, Paul contrasts the wisdom of the world which only sees externals (the cross, a symbol of punishment, the failure of a man who said He was King, etc.) with the wisdom of God which sees in the cross a sign of God's saving power and the ultimate Infinite Love.

2. In the gospel reading, a pagan or Gentile is so struck by the

way Jesus dies that the centurion exclaims: "Clearly this man was the Son of God." Mk. 15:39

3. Down through the centuries, the cross has been either an obstacle to faith or a source of faith and salvation. Countless examples are recorded of people being converted through the power of the cross. Eugene De Mazenod, Founder of the Missionary Oblates of Mary Immaculate, experienced his conversion on Good Friday, 1806, when the cross was unveiled.

4. The power of the cross is there to anyone who is open to its saving power and grace. Salvation is not automatic but demands a personal free act.

5. Tonight we ask you to sign your names to name tags. Before going to confess your sins, we ask you to place that tag on the wooden cross.

6. Why do we ask you to do that? First, to demonstrate that our personal salvation comes about by an act of freely accepting the power of the cross. Jesus died not just for all humankind, but for each of us as individuals. Second, to symbolize that we must die with Jesus to sin by cooperating with the grace of conversion. It's not enough for Jesus to die for our sins, but we also must die *to our sins* — that is, make a firm resolution to change our lives.

III. Examination of Conscience:

A cantor can be used for this examination or it can be recited.

LEADER: For the times that I followed the wisdom of the world rather than the wisdom of the cross.
ALL: Lord, have mercy.
LEADER: For the times I failed to believe in the saving power of your cross.
ALL: Lord, have mercy.
LEADER: For the times I failed to pray to or worship God.
ALL: Lord, have mercy.
LEADER: For the times I disobeyed just laws or showed disrespect for human life in any way.
ALL: Lord, have mercy.
LEADER: For the times I sinfully sought bodily pleasures in thought, word or deed.
ALL: Lord, have mercy.
LEADER: For the times I stole or coveted other's belongings.
ALL: Lord, have mercy.
LEADER: For the times I lied or committed slander or gossiped.
ALL: Lord, have mercy.

LEADER: For the times I failed to respond in love to my neighbor's needs.

ALL: Lord, have mercy.

IV. Song:

"Were You There?" (Negro spiritual)

V. Act of Sorrow:

"Lord, You touched the centurion under the cross to exclaim" "Clearly this man was the Son of God." Likewise you converted Dismas, the thief, so that he gained Paradise the day of your death. Touch us in like manner so that we too might experience Your love on the cross. May we repent of our sins and resolve to sin no more through the power of your cross. Amen."

VI. Symbolic Action of Reconciliation and Absolution

A. The cross is brought to the center aisle by two acolytes and held in such a way that penitents may easily approach the cross. The penitents first approach the cross and place their name tags upon the cross.

B. After the name tags are placed on the cross, the penitents go to the priest or priests for confession and absolution. During a non-sacramental penitential celebration, the priest imposes hands upon each penitent.

VII. Song of Peace:

(The following song is used during the sign of peace): "Peace Is Flowing Like a River" by Carey Landry

VIII. Common Penance:

Sometime during the week, look at a cross in your home and spend a few minutes meditating on Jesus' love in saving you.

IX. Concluding Song:

"Praise The Lord, My Soul" by John Foley, S.J.

Suggestions:

1. We suggest that the cross be a plain wooden cross. In the Holy Family Reconciliation Service, we placed the cross on the altar so that it could dominate the sanctuary.

2. The name tags should be pressure-sensitive to be easily removed. We suggest there be a sufficient number of people in the vestibule prior to the service to help people sign their first names only to the name tags.

3. The priest leading the service might suggest that people try to place the name tags on the cross so as to cover the entire surface. This can be very impressive visually as the cross is raised once more on the altar.

The following appropriate songs may be used for this service:
"Earthen Vessels" by John Foley, S.J.
"I Lift Up My Soul" by Tim Manion
"Take, Lord, Receive" by John Foley, S.J.
"Only This I Want" by Dan Schutte, S.J.
"Redeemer Lord" by John Foley, S.J.

Part III
Pentecost

Theme: Healing And Power Through The Spirit

Dominant Symbol: *Novena Card*

"Receive the Holy Spirit. If you forgive men's sins, they are forgiven them." (Jn. 20:23)

I. Introduction:

A. The theme is announced by the lector: If the church and her individual members could be compared to a boat sailing through eternity, then Christ would be the Master, or in this case, the Pilot, since He is the Way to the Father. It is Christ and his Gospel that show the direction we are to take — this is represented by the map and steering wheel in the sanctuary. But the boat would never sail if there were no wind to be its power, nor could the wind do anything if the sail were bound to the mast. It is the Spirit who gives the Power and it is this same Spirit who enables us to be "unfettered from our sins."

B. Beginning of the service: celebrants come in quietly from the sacristy. Then two lay ministers come in to light the candlebra and unfurl the sail. The song leader begins singing "Spirit of the Living God Fall Afresh On Me" by Daniel Iverson (Moody Press). Twice.

1. Melt me/us
2. Mold me/us
3. Fill me/us
4. Use me/us

Spirit of the Living God fall afresh on me/us.

Then the choir joins the leader in singing and later the congregation is invited to join in for the third time.

C. Opening Prayer: "God, Our Father, You have molded all of us into your image. Help me to melt away our impurities so that we may be filled wth your spirit of love. Use us to further your kingdom of peace and serenity. We ask this through our Lord. Amen."

II. Melt Us:

A. Liturgy of the Word: (*Be seated*)

1. John 3:5-8 (The Holy Spirit gives new life through baptism and is described in the image of wind.)

2. Sequence: (Congregation recites together — remain seated) Come, Holy Spirit/share with us the light of your wisdom/Come, give nourishment to those in need/Come, source of all our gifts/illuminator of our awareness. Come, master of consolation/gentle companion of our life within/fall on us afresh. In the midst of our busy work, Spirit/keep us still within/Bring to our heated moments your cooling touch/Console us when we grieve. Spirit, wonder-full of light/Find the hidden corners of our somehow faithful hearts/Fill them with You. Without your nearness, what is most human in us tends to falter/and our weakness prevails. Come, Holy Spirit, renew our strength/Send your rain down to our dry roots/Heal us where we hurt. Massage the stiffness of our minds/Put your warmth to the coldness in us/Give aim to our wanderings. Gift us, Holy Spirit, with those seven attitudes of yours/Keep alive our faith and hope in you/Awaken our taste for virtue/Open new doors to our freedom/Keep us constant in joyful growth. Amen./

3. Acts 1:12-14 and Acts 2:1-4 (The Holy Spirit descends on the Church with Power.)

4. John 20:19-23 *(Stand)* (Jesus gives the apostles the Spirit and enables them to become instruments of forgiveness.)

> • On Pentecost, the Spirit is associated with images of power — wind and fire. It is the Spirit that gives us the power to change ourselves, the power to change the world.

> • But it is Jesus who gave us The Way or is The Way. he gave us the map for the journey of life. However, without the power of the Spirit, we cannot make the journey.

> • The Church Fathers loved to compare the church to a ship, and the Spirit to the power to fill the sails and move the ship.

> • In the Gospel, we see John's Pentecost — the coming of the Spirit of the Apostles. That coming brings the power to forgive. It is also the Spirit who purifies and brings the Father's forgiveness to this world: first in Baptism and secondly in the Sacrament of Reconciliation.

> • There is a powerful tradition of prayer connected with Pentecost: 1) In the Scriptures, the small church prays for the coming of the Spirit. 2) In the church, we have a tradition of the nine day novena, praying nine days before the feast of Pentecost

● Our symbol tonight is a prayer card to the Holy Spirit.
We ask you to use that prayer for the "communal penance"
and for the days preceding Pentecost.

B. Examination of Conscience" (*Remain seated*)

LEADER: Lord, like your apostles we are weak and sinful, needing your healing forgiveness . . .

ALL: Melt us and make us open to your spirit.

LEADER: Like Peter, we have boasted and relied on our own strength instead of praying and relying on your grace . . .

ALL: Melt us and make us open to your spirit.

LEADER: Like Thomas, we have stubbornly doubted your risen presence in Your Word, the Eucharist, the poor, the handicapped . . .

ALL: Melt us and make us open to your spirit.

LEADER: Like Judas, we have at times betrayed You because of our love for power, money . . .

ALL: Melt us and make us open to your spirit.

LEADER: Like James and John, we have sometimes looked for prestige, wanting to sit at the right hand of power . . .

ALL: Melt us and make us open to your spirit.

LEADER: Like the apostles, we may bicker and quarrel, fight and become jealous of another's good fortune . . .

ALL: Melt us and make us open to your spirit.

LEADER: Like James and John, we want to call down that fire of your vengeance upon sinners, instead of Your infinite forgiveness . . .

ALL: Melt us and make us open to your spirit.

LEADER: Like Peter, we come to You asking, "Lord, What is in it for us?," instead of trusting your generosity . . .

ALL: Melt us and make us open to your spirit.

LEADER: Like Judas, at times we close ourselves off to your forgiveness and retreat into loneliness or despair . . .

ALL: Melt us and make us open to your spirit.

III. Mold Us:

A. Act of Sorrow: (*Please kneel, pray together*)

"Lord, at times we are like the apostles in the Upper Room/awaiting the healing power of your spirit./ Like those apostles, we have guilt and fear/ we feel the guilt of cowardice or greed/ or betrayal or jealousy, or desire for power/ We feel frightened, alone and helpless,/ unable to bring the Good News to others because of our own brokenness/ We ask, O Lord for the Spirit, to heal us with the balm of forgiveness/ We seek the power of the Spirit/ that makes us bold to carry the Good News to others/ Amen."

B. Receiving the Symbols of Reconciliation and Absolution:

1. We ask each person to come forward down the center aisle. The penitent confesses and the priests place hands on the head of each penitent as a sign of forgiveness and then gives him or her absolution. In case of the use of non-sacramental penitential celebration, simply impose hands and say, "May the Spirit heal you and give you power."

2. The penitent then moves over to the liturgical assistant and receives the Holy Spirit Novena Card and returns to pew by the side aisle. (Choir sings songs at this time.)

IV. Fill Us:

A. Sign of Peace: (*Stand*)
"Peace Is Flowing Like A River" by Carey Landry

B. Common Penance: Use Novena prayer card as directed by priest. Recite "Come Holy Spirit."

V. Use Us:

    A. Choir will sing refrain only of "The Spirit Is A Movin' " by Carey Landry.

    B. Matthew 28:16-20 is read by the priest while the choir hums the above song.

    C. People join with choir in singing "The Spirit Is A Movin'" by Carey Landry.

Suggestions:

    1. The decor includes a map, steering wheel and a Gospel book and a home-made mast and sail. At the beginning of the service, a quiet fan causes the sail to fill out.

    2. The prayer card can be purchased at a very reasonable price from Concordia Publishing House, 3558 S. Jefferson Ave., St. Louis, MO 63118.

    3. The following appropriate songs may also be used for this service:
"City of God" by Dan Schutte, S.J.
"He Has Anointed Me" by Balhoff, Ducote, Daigle
"Lord, Send Out Your Spirit" by Balhoff, Ducote, Daigle
"Spirit of God" by Gregory Norbet, O.S.B. (Weston Priory)

Part IV
General

Theme: Slay The Dragons In Your Life

Dominant Symbol: *Paper Dragons*

"Those who belong to Christ Jesus have crucified their flesh with its passions and desires." (Gal. 5:24)

Theme: (To be read by a lector)

"Because of original sin, our human nature has been wounded and weakened. Within all of us are demons and dragons that we label tonight as the 'Seven Capital Sins — pride, envy, anger, gluttony, lust, greed and sloth.' However, each individual, although beset by all seven sins, usually experiences one sin that is stronger and more troublesome than the others. Tonight we want you to look at all seven dragons; however, we also want you to focus in on those particular dragons that tend to dominate your lives. Then with the *power of Christ's love*, the Spirit, we pray that those dragons in our lives may be slain or rendered harmless."

I. Introduction:

A. As the priests come down the center aisle with two acolytes bearing candles, the following song is sung: "If God Is For Us" by John Foley, S.J. The priest goes to his place in the sanctuary and the acolytes place their candles in an appropriate place.

B. Opening Prayer: "Heavenly Father, we come together tonight to face the dragons of sin within us. Give us the courage to examine honestly the dark caverns of our hearts and fill us with the power of your love so that we may conquer the dragons within us. We ask this through Jesus who has conquered sin and death. Amen."

II. Liturgy of the Word:

A. Colossians 3:5-9: (Need to put to death whatever in your being is rooted in earth)

B. Response: "Remember Your Love" by Balhoff, Ducote, Daigle

C. Romans 8:35-39: (Who will separate us from Christ's love?)

D. The congregation is asked to sing the refrain, "Speak Lord, I'm Listening. Plant your word down deep in me. Speak Lord, I'm Listening. Please show me the way." (from "Speak, Lord" by Gary Ault)

E. Gospel: Mark 7:20-23 (What emerges from within renders us impure.)

F. Homily Hints:

1. The legend of St. George killing the dragon is a symbol of the Christian struggle against evil and sin. (It may be good to recall that legend with the congregation.)

2. But not all the dragons are found in social structures or outside ourselves. The sins we find in the social structures begin with the sins we find within ourselves. The dragons are within. For instance, the poverty found in the ghettoes is not due to the poverty found in the United States, but to the greed of the people.

3. The church lists seven capital sins as the major sins or obstacles to the life of God within us. Tonight we concentrate on these seven dragons.

4. Although we all experience these seven dragons, we usually have a dominant dragon or sin that tends to control our lives.

5. Slaying the dragon is not a one-time struggle. There is a certain sorcery within that gives new life to that dragon when we least expect it or we let our guard down. Complacency is the most dangerous thing for a Christian, as the Saints would tell us.

6. Although fear of hell and purgatory were the primary motives for conquering sin in the pre-Vatican II days, we now emphasize the power of Christ's love, or the Spirit, as the most dynamic way of being victorious over the dragon of sin.

7. Throughout the ages, writers and dramatists have played up the age-old struggle between the power of evil and the power of love, of darkness and light. Even in the film "Star Wars," the heroes say: "May the force be with you!" In a way, we can say tonight: "May God's Spirit, his power, his force be with you."

III. Examination of Conscience:

The priest or lector can lead the people in the Examination of Conscience.

LEADER: Because of my Dragon of Pride do I use others in order to get what I want? Do I achieve for myself, no matter what the cost, losing all care ad concern for others? Does this dragon lead to ambition, hypocrisy, lying, and cheating, so that I can be "number one" or the center of things: (Pause) Let us pray . . .

ALL: Lord, send your power of love to slay the dragon.

LEADER: Does the power of the Dragon of Envy stunt my

growth? Do I spend my time carrying and nurturing resentments and grudges? Do I have ill feelings because others have good fortune? Do I allow this dragon to make me happy when others experience misfortune? (Pause) Let us Pray . . .

ALL: Lord, send your power of love to slay the dragon.

LEADER: Does the Dragon of Anger cut me off from others by fighting, by harsh words and insults? Do I refuse to love others, forgive and reach out because I refuse to control or let go of my angry feelings? (Pause) Let us Pray . . .

ALL: Lord, send your power of love to slay the dragon.

LEADER: Does the Dragon of Intemperance make me gluttonous for food, for drink, for the comfortable life? Have I become lazy and apathetic about my spiritual and physical well being because of this dragon having power in my life? (Pause) Let us Pray . . .

ALL: Lord, send your power of love to slay the dragon.

LEADER: How does the Dragon of Pleasure-seeking show itself in my life? Does this force lead me to say that anything is O.K. because it makes me feel good? Do I respect my body and the bodies of others or do I engage in selfish pleasures thereby, showing a lack of consideration for myself and others? (Pause) Let us Pray . . .

ALL: Lord, send your power of love to slay the dragon.

LEADER: Does the power of the Dragon of Greed keep me from caring about the poor, the lonely, the neglected? Am I too busy seeking my own wealth, position, comfort, to work at being part of the community and caring about others? Am I unduly anxious about material possessions and unwilling to share? (Pause) Let us Pray . . .

ALL: Lord, send your power of love to slay the dragon.

LEADER: Do I allow the Dragon of Laziness to make me lukewarm and indifferent? Do I avoid the task of personal and spiritual growth because it is too much work? Do I refuse to answer God's call in my life to change and to care about others because I won't put forth the effort or because I have the attitude that someone else can do it? Do I slack off in my responsibilities to be of service to others at home or in the civic and church communities? (Pause) Let us Pray . . .

ALL: Lord, send your power of love to slay the dragon.

IV. Act of Repentance and Reconciliation: *(All kneel and recite)*

"Almighty and merciful God, we confess that we have sinned. We are sorry for offending You. You have brought us together to receive your mercy and grace, to be forgiven to change our lives. Where the Dragons of Sin have divided us, broken us, and made us weak let your power of love unite, heal and strengthen us to grow. Give us the courage and conviction to change, to love, to rid our lives of its dragons and live a new life . . . one that reflects our positive response to your call. We ask this through Christ our Lord. Amen.''

V. Symbolic Action of Reconciliation and Absolution: (*Be seated until it's time to come forward*)

A. The penitent first of all crushes the paper dragon and puts it in a special box held by acolytes standing on either side of the center aisle. (See suggestion two.)

B. The penitent then goes to the priest to confess and receive absolution, or if the non-sacramental penitential celebration is used, the priest imposes hands on each penitent.

VI. Common Penance:

The priest and congregation now recite the words of St. Paul together as a common penance:

"Those who belong to Christ Jesus have crucified their flesh with its passions and desires. Since we live by the spirit, let us follow the spirit's lead. Let us never be boastful, or challenging or jealous toward one another." (Gal. 5:24-26)

VII. Concluding Song: "Mighty Lord" by John Foley, S.J.

Suggestions:

1. For the decor in the sanctuary, the Holy Family Parish made seven large cut-outs of dragons in different colors to represent the different sins. (For example, green for "envy," and red for "anger") On each dragon was written the name of the corresponding sin.

2. Secondly, we gave small cut-outs of dragons to each person upon entering the church. These were crushed and discarded as indicated in the service.

3. We might suggest that the priest, in the homily, point out these seven dragons on the sanctuary wall. Banners can also be used in place of the cut-outs.

4. The following songs could also be used in this service:
"Be Not Afraid" by Bob Dufford, S.J.
"For You Are My God" by John Foley, S.J.
"Sing To The Mountains" by Bob Dufford, S.J.
"City Of God" by Daniel Schutte, S.J.
"Song Of Thanksgiving" by Darryl Ducote

Theme: Surrender To the Lord

Dominant Symbol" *Key*

"If anyone hears me calling and opens the door, I will enter his house." (Rv. 3:20)

I. Introduction: (*Read by lector*).

Because of original sin we all struggle with certain compulsions to sin varying with each individual. It is only through the power of Jesus Christ that we are liberated from these compulsions. The most important step is surrendering to the power of Jesus in our lives. Alcoholics Anonymous has taught us that there are 12 steps in the conversion of an alcoholic and these can be applied to all the compulsions. Tonight we apply these 12 steps to the spiritual preparation and reception of the sacrament of Reconciliation.

II. Entrance:

While the congregation or choir sing the antiphon, the priest or priests begin to incense the congregation. A lector leads the people in the recitation of Psalm 51, interspersed with the singing of the antiphon, preferably by the choir. The priests go down the center aisle and side aisles, incensing the people.

Antiphon: Come, O Lord, and set us free. Bring your people peace. Come, O Lord, and set us free. Come, Lord Jesus, Come.

Song: "Come, O Lord" by Ducotte, Daigle.

After the incensing, the priest goes to his seat in the sanctuary.

III. Opening Prayer:

"O Lord, we are powerless before the compulsions of sin without your healing grace. Help us to open our hearts so that we may surrender to You and receive the power of the Spirit to be truly free. Amen."

IV. Liturgy of the Word:

Step 1: *I am powerless*
First Reading: Romans 7:14-23 (Paul's inner struggle with power of evil.)

Step 2: *God can heal me.*
Response: Mathew 5:3-10 (A lector should guide the congregation to recite the Beatitudes slowly.)

Step 3: *Surrender to God.*

Second Reading: revelation 3:19b-21 (Only we can open the door to Jesus.)

V. Homily Hints:

A. Through original sin, we have lost some of our freedom as human beings. Left to ourselves we would become slaves of compulsions such as lust, greed, pride, power, etc.

B. Paul openly speaks of his helplessness before power of flesh. (Rom. 7:14-23)

C. Paul then says that only Jesus can liberate us from this slavery. (Rom. 7:24-25)

It is by surrendering to Jesus that we open up to the power of the Spirit. We, however, hold the key to our hearts. (Familiar painting of Jesus knocking at the door of the heart with no handle on the outside and which can be opened only from the inside.)

D. But Jesus respects freedom and will never force us to open the door.

E. For the addiction of alcoholism, AA has developed 12 steps and surrender is step three. But the 12 steps present the larger plan of basic Christian living and has been used with great success with the compulsions of fear and overeating and smoking.

F. Those 12 steps are being used tonight as the steps of conversion involved when we receive the sacrament of Reconciliation.

G. We are giving you a card tonight with the famous Serenity Prayer used by Alcoholic Anonymous. The key attached to the card represents the key to the heart — only the individual person can open the door to Jesus. You alone possess the key.

VI. Examination of Conscience:

(After each petition respond: Come, O Lord, and set us free.) Each petition is introduced by a leader of prayer.

Step 4: *Examine my life.*

LEADER: From the need to criticize and judge others . . .
ALL: Come, O Lord, and set us free.
LEADER: From the need to nurse and hold onto grudges and hurts of the past . . .
ALL: Come, O Lord, and set us free.
LEADER: From the need to keep up with the Joneses, no matter the price . . .
ALL: Come, O Lord, and set us free.

Step 5: *Confess my sins.*

> LEADER: From the need to dominate in conversation and to spread gossip . . .
> ALL: Come, O Lord, and set us free.
> LEADER: From the driving need to overspend . . .
> ALL: Come, O Lord, and set us free.

Step 6: *Let go of the past:*

> LEADER: From the compulsive need for sexual pleasure . . .
> ALL: Come, O Lord, and set us free.
> LEADER: From the crippling fear of being rejected by others or of failing . . .
> ALL: Come, O Lord, and set us free.
> LEADER: From alcoholic or other chemical addiction . . .
> ALL: Come, O Lord, and set us free.

Step 7: *Beg God to heal me.*

> LEADER: From the excessive need to meet others' approval or the excessive fear of being hurt . . .
> ALL: Come, O Lord, and set us free.
> LEADER: From self-built walls that isolate us from others . . .
> ALL: Come, O Lord, and set us free.

Step 8: *Recall all those I've harmed:*

> PRIEST: O Lord, we ask you to free us from domination of sin and to give us a new liberty from all compulsion. We desire to let go of the past and to amend the harm we have caused. We find the power to do this in Jesus Christ, Our Savior, Amen.

VII. Act of Sorrow: (kneel and recite together)

"Lord Jesus, You opened the eyes of the blind, healed the sick, forgave the sinful woman, and after Peter's denial, confirmed him in your love. Listen to my prayer: forgive all my sins, renew your love in my heart, help me to live in harmony with my neighbors that I may proclaim your saving power to all the world."

VIII. Receiving the Symbol and Absolution:

A. The congregation is asked to come forward and confess and receive absolution. The priest will place his hands on the penitent's head.

B. Then the penitent goes to a minister on either side to receive a serenity prayer card with the symbolic "key" attached.

C. Various songs may be used but the most appropriate song is given below. Song: "Lay Your Hands" by Carey Landry.

IX. Common Penance: *Priest gives the penance*

Step 9: *Make amends if possible.*
People read from the symbolic card the Prayer of Serenity. (*All kneel*)

Step 10: *Live one day at a time.*
Priest asks people to make silently a firm resolution to commit their lives to Christ.

Step 11: *Stay strong by prayer/meditation.*
People give to others a sign of peace. (*All stand*)
Song during Sign of Peace: "Peace is Flowing like a River" by Carey Landry.

X. Conclusion:

Step 12: *Carry the message to others*
Final exhortation
Concluding Song: "Sing a New Song Unto the Lord" by Dan Schutte, S.J.

Suggestions:

1. The decor for the service could highlight the 12 steps of AA by designing 12 large tag-board signs in the shape of keys listing the 12 steps. A large advent wreath is placed in a prominent position in the sanctuary. This service could easily by used for retreats for AA or for any other time of the year.

2. A Prayer of Serenity card can be obtained through any AA catalogue or Religious Supply Co. We collected old keys from parishoners and attached the key to the prayer card. We asked them to hang the symbol on their Christmas trees.

3. The following appropriate songs may be used in this service:
"You Are Near" by Dan Schutte, S.J.
"Beatitudes" by Balhoff, Ducote

COMMUNAL RECONCILIATION SERVICE NUMBER 12

Theme: Judge Not, Lest You Be Judged

Dominant Symbol: *Stones*

"Let the man among you who has no sin be the first to cast a stone at her." (Jn. 8:7)

Theme: (To be read by a lector before the service begins.) "Jesus was very insistent in the Gospels that we not be judgmental people. Instead of judging other people, he asks us to look at our own hearts and at our own sins. His stance toward sinful people is one of compassion and mercy rather than condemnation. If He became angry, it was only with the proud, the hypocritical, the self-righteous, and the legalistic."

I. Introduction:

A. The priests enter from the sacristy during the following opening song: "I Lift Up My Soul" by Tim Manion.

B. Opening Prayer: "Heavenly Father, let us see through our need to judge others. We came tonight not to judge others but to look at our own sinfulness. Strip us of our hypocrisy, our self-righteousness, so that we may see ourselves as we are and thus open our hearts to your forgiving and healing love. We ask this through Christ our Brother and Savior. Amen."

II. Liturgy of the Word:

A. Ezekiel 11:17-21 (God will take away our stony hearts and replace them with hearts of flesh.)

B. Response: (Recite the refrain after each verse)
Give me back the joy of your salvation.

> LEADER: A clean heart create for me, O God . . .
> ALL: Give me back the joy of your salvation
> LEADER: And a steadfast spirit renew within me . .
> ALL: Give me back the joy of your salvation
> LEADER: Cast me not out from your presence . . .
> ALL: Give me back the joy of your salvation
> LEADER: And your Holy Spirit take not from me . . .
> ALL: Give me back the joy of your salvation
> LEADER: Give me back the joy of your salvation . .

58

ALL: Give me back the joy of your salvation.
LEADER: And a willing spirit sustain in me . . .
ALL: Give me back the joy of your salvation.

C. 1 Corinthians 4:1-5 (Stop passing judgment on others.) (*Short silence after reading*)

D. Gospel: John 8:3-11 (Jesus forgives the woman taken in adultery.)

E. Homily Hints:
1. This Gospel reading was an embarrassment to the early Christians who were almost scandalized at Jesus forgiving a woman caught in adultery.

2. The Pharisees in this story are not concerned about the double standard of morality (the man who committed adultery with her is not condemned here); nor are they concerned with a woman changing her life. They are merely using her and the law to get at Jesus.

3. Jesus doesn't deny the law nor condone the act. Rather, he merely places a mirror of their own sinfulness before them. Somehow He confronts their hypocrisy and self-righteousness. How does He do this? Some commentators say that He wrote their secret sins in sand.

4. In shamefulness, they walked away, one by one.

5. It is our own stony hearts, as Ezechiel says, that can become the villains. Because our hearts become hard and judgmental, and self-righteous, we no longer see our own sins or we rationalize them away.

6. What is it in us that wants to be judge? One of the first acts of Adam after the fall was to put the blame on Eve and rationalize his own disobedience. We have been doing that down through the ages. In a sense, it is our desire to play God, to play the perfect being.

7. In the Gospel, Jesus showed God's heart — a heart that seeks to forgive and to allow conversion rather than to condemn.

8. What would Jesus write in the sand if we asked Him about *our* sins? That's the question tonight. We are not asking Him to write the sins of others, but *my* sins. In AA, they say, "Don't take anybody else's inventory. Just take your own."

9. When you entered tonight, we gave you a stone. We ask that you not throw it at others, but rather toss it in the metal container before you confess your sins. Throwing the stone aside symbolizes your willingness not to judge others but rather to face up to yourself.

III. Examination of Conscience: (*To be led by priest or lector*)

LEADER: Lord, for the times I have found excuses for not going to Mass or for not praying . . .

ALL: Jesus, write in the sand of my heart that I may see myself.

LEADER: Lord, for the times I hated gossip about myself and yet talked so freely about other's faults . . .

ALL: Jesus, write in the sand of my heart that I may see myself.

LEADER: Lord, for the times I lied in order to save myself embarrassment or correction by others . . .

ALL: Jesus, write in the sand of my heart that I may see myself.

LEADER: Lord, for the times I have played God and judged without knowing the circumstances . . .

ALL: Jesus, write in the sand of my heart that I may see myself.

LEADER: Lord, for the times I have been quick to condemn thieves and yet have cheated on income tax or taken things from the factory or office . . .

ALL: Jesus, write in the sand of my heart that I may see myself.

LEADER: Lord, for the times I have expected one moral standard of women while condoning another standard for men . . .

ALL: Jesus, write in the sand of my heart that I may see myself.

LEADER: Lord, for the times I have been so proud of obeying civil law while neglecting God's law of charity and compassion . . .

ALL: Jesus, write in the sand of my heart that I may see myself.

IV. Act of Sorrow: (*Recite them together, kneeling*)

LEADER: My brothers and sisters, confess your sins and pray for each other that you may be healed.

ALL: I confess to almighty God, and to you, my brothers and sisters, that I have sinned through my own fault in my thoughts and in my words, in what I have done, and in what I have failed to do; and I ask blessed Mary, ever virgin, all the angels and saints, and you, my brothers and sisters, to pray for me to the Lord our God.

V. Symbolic Action of Reconciliation and Absolution:

A. Each penitent comes down the center aisle and tosses his/her stone into a metal container. Preferably it would be a container that would resound as the stones were thrown in.

B. Then the penitent confesses his/her sins and receives absolution. If the non-sacramental penitential celebration is used, the priest imposes hands on each penitent.

VI. Common Penance:

As we say the Our Father as our common penance, let us think of the person we judge most harshly. Let us especially remember the words: "Forgive us our trespasses as we forgive those who trepass against us."

VII. Sign of Peace:

As the sign of peace is given throughout the church, the following song is sung: "Father of peace" by Michael Lynch (Raven).

VIII. Concluding Song:

"Praise The Lord, My Soul" by John Foley, S.J.

Suggestions:

1. For the decor, a sandbox could be placed in the front of the sanctuary with a simulation of Aramaic written in the sand. Sea shells and nets could be used as part of the larger decor.

2. The white decorative stones which were given to people as they entered church were an inexpensive kind of stone which is placed in yards around shrubbery.

3. The following appropriate songs may also be used for this service:
"If God Is For Us" by John Foley, S.J.
"All The Ends Of The Earth" by Robert Dufford, S.J.
"Awaken My Heart" by Lucien Deiss
"Sing Alleluia, Sing" by Gary Ault

COMMUNAL RECONCILIATION SERVICE NUMBER 13

Theme: Commit Yourself to Jesus, Your friend

Dominant Image: *The Altar*

"There is no greater love than this: to lay down one's life for one's friend." (JN 15:13)

Theme: (Read by priest or lector) "A saint is someone who has accepted the friendship of Jesus, and committed himself or herself to follow Jesus, the Master and Lord. Sin is a failure in that friendship and also a backing off of our commitment to Jesus as Lord. For Jesus said, we'd be his friends if we did what He commanded us.

I. Introduction:

A. The priest or priests and two acolytes come down the center aisle with lit incense and two candles. During the procession, the following song is sung.

"My Friends, I Bless You" by Gregory Norbet, O.S.B. (Weston Priory)

B. After the song, the priest incenses the altar. During the incensing he says: "Bless this altar, O Lord, Heavenly Father, as a symbol of Jesus Christ, who dies for us as a victim of sin. May it evoke from us the commitment to follow Jesus as Master, even unto the cross." Amen.

C. Opening Prayer:

Priest: "Let us pray. (pause) Loving Father, You do not desire the death of the sinner, but rather You wish to see us reconciled with You in friendship. For You are, indeed, our Friend. When we fall, You are there to support us. When we forget, you gently remind us. When we cease to be your friend, you go out of your way to re-establish a loving relationship with us. May we be open to your love. May we find in the saints models for our lives, that we may be devoted to you, not out of fear or guilt, but out of love and friendship. We ask this through Jesus Christ who is Love Incarnate. Amen."

II. Liturgy of the Word:

A. Exodus 19:3-6 (You shall be my special people.)

B. Response: (There should be a short period of silence.)

C. John 15:9-15: (You are no longer my servants but my friends.)

D. Homily Hints:

1. What does it mean to be a Christian?

   • It means to accept Jesus Christ as Master and Lord. He becomes "number one" in your life.

   • It means accepting God not just as all-powerful, but as a human friend in Jesus.

   • It means accepting Jesus' message of what He has to say to us.

2. Even though we were baptized as children, it does not mean we have committed ourselves as adults to Jesus Christ. Consequently, this is an on-going process.

3. Although we may have been serious about our commitment to Jesus and our friendship with Him, we sometimes fail as weak human beings. This means we fail in our friendship with Jesus and back away from our commitment. The saints, too, had these struggles.

4. If Jesus seems far away from us, we must ask the question: "Who moved?"

5. From earliest times, the altar has been a symbol of Christ and the priest in kissing the altar, also shows his love for Jesus.

6. Tonight we ask you to renew your friendship with and commitment to Jesus Christ as "number one" in your life. You will do that symbolically by touching the altar before confessing your sins to the priest.

7. We must remember that Jesus' friendship never ends. Even with Judas, Jesus offered his friendship and forgiveness. Jesus' own words remind us of this. "There is no greater love than this: To lay down one's life for one's friends." (Jn 15:13)

III. Examination of Conscience: (*Remain seated*)

LEADER: Let us look at ourselves and discover whether or not we have really understood what Jesus meant when He called us to friendship. To the various petitions in the Examination of Conscience, please respond, Forgive us, Lord.

LEADER: You have called us to friendship, Lord . . . but we have turned to idols . . . idols of pleasure and power and popularity and possessions . . . (pause) We pray:

ALL: Forgive us, Lord.

LEADER: You have called us to friendship, Lord . . . but we have been deaf to your Word Sunday after Sunday . . . (pause) We pray:

ALL: Forgive us, Lord.

LEADER: You have called us to friendship, Lord . . . but we have been cold, hard, indifferent and uncaring at times . . . (pause) We pray:

ALL: Forgive us, Lord.

LEADER: You have called us to friendship, Lord . . . and yet we have rejected You in others by condemning and hurting them in our words and deeds . . . (pause) We pray:

ALL: Forgive us, Lord.

LEADER: You have called us to friendship, Lord . . . but we have been distrustful of You, or critical or afraid of what You might ask of us . . . (pause) We pray:

ALL: Forgive us, Lord.

LEADER: You have called us to friendship, Lord . . . but we haven't worked for your kingdom as You've asked us to do . . . (pause) We pray:

ALL: Forgive us, Lord.

LEADER: Let us kneel as a sign of our sorrow for our lack of response to the Lord's call to friendship and recite this act of contrition, of sorrow for our sins.

IV. Act of Sorrow:

All: Loving Lord, we're sorry for the many times we have failed to build a real friendship with You. We have closed our ears to Your Word. We have broken Your law. We have lived as a people without Your saving promise. We have not loved. Help us have a change of heart, a true and lasting inner conversion. Bring us, by the power of the Spirit, back to the Word, the Law and the Promise. Bring us back to friendship with You.

V. Song: "Hosea" by Gregory Norbet, O.S.B. (Weston Priory).

VI. Symbolic Action of Reconciliation and Absolution:

A. First, the penitents go to the center aisle and, two by two, touch the altar, pausing for a moment to make a commitment to Christ.

B. After the commitment, the penitents go to the priest or priests for confession and absolution. In case of a non-sacramental Penitential Celebration, the priest imposes hands on the head of each penitent.

VII. Sign of Peace:

Use the following song during the sign of peace. (It is a good time to emphasize that good friends shake hands or kiss, as the custom may be.)

"The Peace of the Lord" by Gary Ault

VIII. Common Penance:

To be a friend of Jesus is to be a friend with one another. Choose to mend one friendship that needs mending. Here are some suggested ways to do so.

- On this day, mend a quarrel
- Write a love letter
- Encourage youth in a special way
- Forego a grudge
- Forgive an enemy
- Listen to someone needing an understanding ear
- Examine your demands on others
- Express your gratitude to someone
- Gladden the heart of a child

IX. Concluding Song:

"City of God" by Dan Schutte, S.J.

Suggestions:

1. The tie-in between commitment to Jesus, symbolized by the altar, and commitment to Sunday worship, is also possible.

2. The following appropriate songs could be used for this service:
"I Will Sing of the Lord" by John Foley, S.J.
"Sing a New Song" by Dan Schutte, S.J.
"Here I Am, Lord" by Dan Schutte, S.J.
"In His People Everywhere" by Joe Pinson

COMMUNAL RECONCILIATION SERVICE NUMBER 14

Theme: You Are The Potter; We Are The Clay
"O Lord, you are our Father; we are the clay and you the potter: we are all the work of your hands." (Is. 64:7)

Dominant Symbol: *Clay pots*

I. Introduction:

A. A half hour before the service begins, a potter is fashioning a pot in the sanctuary. A minute or so before the service begins, a minister comes with hot charcoal to place in the clay pot just previously fashioned. The potter puts incense in the finished pot and retires to the sacristy.

B. Theme: (*Announced by the lector*)
We need to be like clay in God's hands. The Father, as the potter, *formed* us in his own image and likeness at Baptism. But He doesn't stop there. Because we are prodigal children, God continues to *reform* us throughout our lives, but especially when we gather for the sacrament of Reconciliation.

C. Entrance: As the choir sings the first verse of "Abba Father," a procession begins with two candle bearers and two priests. In the middle section of the church, eight lay people of varying ages are seated in the congregation in different pews holding clay pots of varied sizes. The vases are to represent different Christians in their individual uniqueness. The lay people stand and join in the procession as the candle bearers pass by their pews. Finally the priests join the procession from the rear of the church. Song: "Abba Father" by Carey Landry.

D. Opening Prayer: The lay people return to their pews and the priests go to their chairs in the sanctuary. The presider opens with a prayer: "O Heavenly Father, You *created* Adam and Eve out of clay like the master-potter that You are and You *recreated* us through Baptism in the image of Jesus Christ. You have formed us and now we ask You to reform us through the work of the Holy Spirit. Amen."

II. Liturgy of the Word: (*Be seated*)

A. Genesis 2:4-7 (The story of God's creation of man and woman from the clay of the earth.)

B. Repeat in song: "Abba Father, you are the potter, we are the clay, the work of Your hands" (Carey Landry). Invite people to stand with open hands in the spirit of docility and receptivity of God's Word.

C. Jeremiah 18:1-7 (God the potter can always reform his creation no matter how broken we are through sin.)

D. 2 Corinthians 4:1-7 (This treasure of Christ we possess in earthen vessels.)

III. Homily Hints:

A. Emphasize the image of God as potter in creation.

B. Explain the opening scenario of the potter at the wheel. Point out the symbolism of the potter and *The Clay*. The potter is God the creator; we are the clay.

C. The hands of the potter must be sensitive and form each pot individually signifying the uniqueness of each individual.

D. The potter needs water for pliability to fashion the pot. Our Baptism should keep us open and pliable to the work of the Holy Spirit.

E. The clay, unlike stone, is fragile and pliable and can be fashioned by the potter.

F. The finished pot, however, remains clay and not steel. It is fragile and can be broken by sin. (2 Corinthians 4:7 emphasizes this)

G. Yet the Master Potter never throws us away but mends us and refashions us, in the sacrament of Reconciliation.

Song: "Spirit of the Living God" by Daniel Iverson.

IV. Examination of Conscience: (*Remain seated*)

LEADER: Sin weakens or breaks our relationship, not only with God but also with others. We carry this treasure of grace in earthen vessels. We can also be responsible for the brokenness of other people. In reconciliation, we ask God to heal our brokenness and to make us instruments in the healing of others. Lord, for the brokenness I experience in times of uncontrolled anger . . . (pause)

ALL: Lord, heal our brokenness.

LEADER: Lord, for the brokenness I experience in the times of unbridled passion . . . (pause)

ALL: Lord, heal our brokenness.

LEADER: Lord, for the brokenness I experience in the times of crass laziness . . . (pause)

ALL: Lord, heal our brokenness.

LEADER: Lord, for the brokenness I experience in times of jealousy and envy . . . (pause)

ALL: Lord, heal our brokenness.

LEADER: Lord, for the brokenness I experience in times of haughty pride . . . (pause)

ALL: Lord, heal our brokenness.

LEADER: Lord, for the brokenness I experience in times of greed . . . (pause)

ALL: Lord, heal our brokenness.

LEADER: Lord, for the brokenness I experience in times of apathy and indifference . . . (pause)

ALL: Lord, heal our brokenness.

LEADER: Lord, for any brokenness I know in the depths of my own heart . . . (longer pause — for quiet reflection)

ALL: Lord, heal our brokenness.

V. Sign of Sorrow: (*Kneel and make an act of sorrow together*)

PRIESTS: Let us pray for God's mercy by the power of the Spirit.

ALL: We confess to almighty God, to Jesus Christ the Lord, and to the whole church of our brothers and sisters, that we have sinned in unloving deeds: By leaving undone what we ought to have done, and by doing what we should have left undone. We ask for mercy and healing for our brokenness. We ask you, Lord, to give us this day the wisdom and courage to begin anew. May our lives truly be a reflection of your love.

VI. Receiving Symbol of Reconciliation and Absolution:

A. We ask each person, beginning with those in the front pews, to approach the priests to confess and receive absolution, or, in case a non-sacramental penitential celebration is used, the priest imposes hands on each of the penitents.

B. The penitents move over to the liturgical assistant, to receive a symbol of reconciliation. They return to their pews and sit. Choir sings several songs during this time.

VII. Sign of Peace: (*Stand*)

"Earthen vessels" by John Foley, S.J.

VIII. Common Penance: (*Remain standing — recite together*) Psalm 103:1-5

Bless the Lord, O my soul; and all my being, bless his holy name.

Bless the Lord, O my soul, and forget not all his benefits.

He pardons all your iniquities, he heals all your ills.

He redeems your life from destruction, he crowns you with kindness and compassion,

He fills your lifetime with good; your youth is renewed like the eagle's.

IX. Concluding Song:

"Sing A New Song" by Dan Schutte, S.J.

Suggestions:

1. If a potter is not available, then clay pots could still be used as a decor and in procession. In that case a clay pot with burning incense could be used in procession.

2. In the Holy Family Parish Service, we asked a potter to make small finger pots to which we attached, by bag twister, small cards on which were printed the words, "Abba Father, You are the potter, we're the clay." The pots could be easily hung in the house or on a Christmas tree.

3. If real clay pots are not given out as symbols, then a picture of a clay pot and key saying of Isaiah, "We are the clay, and you are the potter . . ." (Is. 64:7) might be printed on the card.

4. The following appropriate songs may be used for this service:
"Blessed Be God Forever" by Erich Sylvester
"I Have Loved You" by Michael Joncas
"The Hand of God" by Carey Landry
"In His People Everywhere" by Joe Pinson

COMMUNAL RECONCILIATION SERVICE NUMBER 15

Theme: Be A Living Stone

Dominant Symbol: *The Agate*

"Come to him the living stone . . . You too are living stones." (1 Pt. 2:4-5)

I. Introduction:

A. The theme is announced by the Lector: "Christ invites us to come to Him, the cornerstone on which the church is built. With Christ as the cornerstone and foundation, you and I are the living stones. We are the church, despite our weakness and sinfulness; yet it is precisely our sinfulness that weakens and destroys the church and causes disunity among the living stones. Through forgiveness, Christ rebuilds his church progressively in every age."

B. Beginning of the Service: (*Stand*)

The priests process down the center aisle while the song "Priestly People" is sung. The song leader, as cantor, sings the verses while the congregation joins in singing only the antiphon.

C. The priest now blesses the Christ-Cornerstone and symbols of reconciliation with holy water and incense, using the following blessing:

"Heavenly Father, we ask you to bless this rock, symbol of Jesus Christ, the cornerstone of the church. May Jesus, who is our Savior and the cause of our forgiveness, cleanse his people of all that divides and all that destroys his church. May He continue to unify and hold together his chosen people, the living stones from which He builds his temple. In the name of the Father, the Son, and the Holy Spirit. Amen."

After that, the priest blesses the People of God while other verses of the above song are sung. The priests incense the people down the aisles and return down the center aisle.

D. Opening Prayer: "Let us pray: Father, we come to you tonight as your people that we may again renew our commitment to Jesus the cornerstone and foundation upon which we build. We come as sinful people, knowing that we are still in need of salvation and forgiveness. We come to you, as living stones of your church asking that through the forgiveness and healing of the Spirit, we may continue to build your church, the symbol of the eternal and everlasting Jerusalem. Amen."

II. Liturgy of the Word: (*Be seated*)

A. I Corinthians 3:10-11: (Jesus is the only foundation upon which to build.) (Another possible reading would be Ephesians 2:19-22.)

Song refrain: "If the Lord Does Not Build" by Dan Schutte, S.J.
"If the Lord does not build a house,
then in vain do the builders labor.
And in vain does the watchman stand his
guard, If the Lord is not his help,
if the Lord is not his help."

B. I Peter 2:4-7: (*Stand*) (We are the spiritual stones built upon the foundation of Jesus.)

C. Homily Hints:

1. We seldom think of God as Rock (maybe Father, Shepherd) yet both the Old and New Testament are filled with images of God the Rock.

2. Jesus refers to Himself as the Cornerstone.

3. He names his vicar on earth, Peter the Rock.

4. We build first of all on Jesus Christ the Cornerstone and it is through Jesus that we worship the Father.

5. It is Jesus we encounter in every sacrament.

6. But we, too, are called rocks — "precious stones, redeemed at a great price." It is the Holy Spirit and Christian charity which holds us together like cement holding together precious rocks in the structure of a temple. Sinfulness destroys or at least weakens the structure of the church or mars the beauty of the precious spiritual stones.

7. Jesus through the Holy Spirit forgives us tonight, restores our beauty and strengthens our community the church. We give you an agate as a reminder that we are called to "Be a living stone."

8. Tonight, in a symbolic gesture, as a sign of our personal commitment to Jesus the Cornerstone, we ask you to touch the rock in front of the sanctuary.

9. The priest can illustrate this idea of church by using the child's handplay: "Here's the church, and here's the steeple, open the door and see all the people."

III. Examination of Conscience: (*Remain seated — the church will be darkened*)

Introduction: Sin is destructive of the church. St. Paul reminds us that sin is the opposite of love. Sin does not bind together, but rather separates us from Christ and divides us from one another. There truly is no private sin: every sin hurts my sister and brother and in turn weakens and divides the church. In light of our common sinfulness and our common need for forgiveness, let us now examine our consciences.

LEADER: From our possessiveness . . . which makes us cling to and keep things we do not need . . . free us from sins that weaken and divide your church . . . (pause)

ALL: Deliver us your people.

LEADER: From our selfishness . . . which makes us place ourselves before others, insensitive to the concerns and feelings of our sisters and brothers . . . free us from sins and build us into your Holy People . . . (pause)

ALL: Deliver us your people.

LEADER: From our pride . . . which makes us say we are better than others . . . free us from sins and build us into your Holy People . . . (pause)

ALL: Deliver us your people.

LEADER: From our anger . . . which makes us try to hurt one another and makes it difficult to forgive . . . free us from sins that weaken and divide your church . . . (pause)

ALL: Deliver us your people.

LEADER: From our pride . . . which makes us say we are better than others . . . free us from sins and build us into your Holy People . . . (pause)

ALL: Deliver us your people.

LEADER: From our fears . . . which makes us unable to risk ourselves in our relations with others, unable to face the truth when we encounter it . . . free us from sins and build us into your Holy People . . . (pause)

ALL: Deliver us your people.

LEADER: From our insecurities . . . which cause us to be defensive, unable to come to decisions, or to affirm ourselves or others . . . free us from sins that weaken and divide your church . . . (pause)

LEADER: From our prejudice . . . which makes us judge others superficially . . . free us from sins and builds us into your Holy People . . . (pause)

ALL: Deliver us your people.

LEADER: From our secret sins, known only by ourselves and

God . . . which stand in the way of true forgiveness . . . free us from sins that weaken and divide your church . . . (pause)

ALL: Deliver us your people.

LEADER: From our self-indulgences . . . which make us feel so sorry for ourselves . . . free us from sins that weaken and divide your church . . . (pause)

ALL: Lord, deliver us your people.

IV. Sign of Sorrow: (*Kneel and make an Act of Contrition together.*)

"Let us pray for God's mercy by the power of the Spirit. We confess to Almighty God, to Jesus Christ the Lord, and to the whole church of our brothers and sisters that we have sinned in unloving deeds: by leaving undone what we ought to have done, and by doing what we should have left undone. We ask mercy, healing and forgiveness. We ask You, Lord, to give us this day, the wisdom and courage to begin anew. May our lives truly be a reflection of your love. This we ask in your name. Amen."

V. Receiving the Symbol of Reconciliation and Absolution:

A. We ask each person to come forward down the center aisle and touch the Christ-stone in a gesture of personal commitment. (see suggestion one)

B. Then step in front of one of the priests for confession and absolution. In case of a non-sacramental penitential celebration, the priest imposes hands on each of the penitents.

C. Finally the penitent moves to the acolyte and receives a symbol and then returns to pew by the side aisle.

VI. Sign of Peace: (*Stand*)

"Peace Is Flowing Like A River" by Carey Landry.

VII. Common Penance: (*Stand*)

Congregation will sing: "Our Father."

VIII. Concluding Song:

"Sing To The Mountains" by Bob Dufford, S.J.

Suggestions:

1. A large rock could be put on a decorated table outside the sanctuary in the center aisle so it could easily be approached and touched by the people. A suitable decor could highlight the rock as a dominant symbol.

2. A polished agate could be given to each penitent. An agate could be glued on a card, bearing the words: "Be a Living Stone." We en-

couraged our people to hang such symbols in their homes or on the Christmas tree.

3. The following appropriate songs must be used for this service:
"Blest Be The Lord" by Dan Schutte, S.J.
"If God Is For Us" by John Foley, S.J.
"The House Built on the Rock" by Lucien Deiss
"Lift Up Your Hearts" by Roc O'Connor, S.J.
"Only This I Want" by Dan Schutte, S.J.

COMMUNAL RECONCILIATION SERVICE NUMBER 16

Theme: Salvation Has Come To Your House Today

Dominant Symbol: *The Door*

"Here I stand, knocking at the door." (Rv. 3:20)

Reconciliation is always, first of all, an invitation from God to forgiveness. Secondly, if we accept that invitation, it is, likewise, a celebration of the forgiveness in praise and thanksgiving. In other words, like Zaccheus, we are invited to dine with the Lord, no matter how small or unworthy we are. Christ's invitation to us tonight is as real as it was to Zaccheus 2000 years ago.

I. Introduction

Proclamation — lights darken — trumpet fanfare — a reader comes out from the sacristy to the center of the sanctuary.

A. "Hear ye, hear ye. Whether from the east or west or even beyond — to all from the highways or the by-ways. The Lord, the Savior the King of the Universe invites you to the Banquet of Forgiveness as he did the tax-collector Zaccheus. Behold, He knocks at your door awaiting your response to his offer of 'Amazing Grace.' "

B. Duet will sing the first verse of "Amazing Grace"; the choir will sing the second verse. The choir and congregation will sing the third verse as the lights go on. During this song, the priests process down the center aisle, led by two servers, who place their candles in the appropriate holders. Song: "Amazing Grace" (Traditional)

C. Opening Prayer: (*Stand*)

"O Lord, we rejoice with your over the recovery of the coin that was lost, over the finding of the sheep that strayed away, the return of the Prodigal Son or Daughter who abandoned your home. We come together tonight to acknowledge your invitation to forgiveness and respond with praise and gratitude. Amen."

II. Liturgy of the Word: (*Be seated*)

A. Book of Revelation 3:20-22: God is standing at the door of our home knocking.

B. Response to the reading: "Standing at the Door" — James Berluch (New Canticle)

C. Gospel of Luke 19:1-10 (The story of Zaccheus, a tax-collector who changed). Mime could be used as the story is read.

D. Homily Hints:

1. Zaccheus was a man up a tree in more ways than one. He was also out on a limb, taking a chance and a risk.

> ● He was a social outcast, a tax-collector, hated by his fellow Jews. He probably couldn't have gotten a front view of Jesus if he tried: the crowd wouldn't have let him through.

> ● In modern jargon, he may have had an inferiority complex because of his shortness.

> ● He was a sinner, but not malicious. He was hungry, thirsty, curious, in need of something more.

> ● Later he stands tall and goes beyond the law in giving restitution — he goes beyond justice to love and generosity.

2. It's interesting that Jesus' entrance into Zaccheus' heart was by way of asking for a favor, asking for a free meal. It's an act of charity that opens his heart for conversion. Jesus entered the *heart* of Zaccheus by entering the *hearth*, the home of Zaccheus.

3. Zaccheus was a son of Abraham by birth, but for Jesus that was not enough. He must become a son of Abraham by faith. Salvation and forgiveness come through an *Act of Faith* in our Savior.

4. Zaccheus ends up a changed man. How did it happen? It came because Zaccheus responded to *several* graces.

> ● The *Grace of Desire*: All salvation begins with desire to see or hear Christ. Hunger and thirst for the spiritual is a grace. Even curiosity into spiritual things can be a grace.

> ● The *Grace of Openness*: Christ is standing at the door asking to be invited in, asking to dine with Zaccheus.

> ● The *Grace of Self-Examination*: In the story, we don't see Zaccheus' soul-searching, but we know it had to have happened.

> ● The *Grace of Confession*: Zaccheus admits that he has sinned and offended others.

> ● The *Grace of a Firm Purpose of Amendment*: In the old Baltimore Cathechism, this meant the intention to change and make amends. Zaccheus does just that.

5. Jesus is present tonight and continues his searching and inviting.

• We're all short of stature in some ways and up a tree because of sin.

• *All need to hear Christ's call*: "Come down, even if it means coming down the aisle." In a way, it's an altar call or a faith call.

6. When we say salvation has come to this house, we mean more than to the individual, but also to all of us as a community.

• When you come down from the "Laying on" of hands, the priests ask: "Will you open the door to your heart?" You are to answer, "I will."

• Now as we examine our consciences, we ask one vital question: "Will you open the door of your hearts to grace of self-examination?"

III. Examination of Conscience: (*Please kneel*)

READER 1: Does God respect our freedom?
CHORUS: Christ stands at the door knocking.
READER 2: Does God force the door of your heart open?
CHORUS: Christ stands at the door knocking.
READER 3: Does God, scold, demand, coerce us to respond to Him? God says gently — "I stand at the door knocking."
CHORUS: Christ stands at the door knocking.
READER 1: Does God desire to come at our request as a guest?
CHORUS: Christ stands at the door knocking.
PRIEST or LECTOR: "Let us now open the door of our sinful hearts as we examine our consciences and invite Jesus, the savior, to heal us."
LEADER: Zaccheus *desired* to see Christ and that was grace . . . For the times I stifled my desire for Jesus by refusing to pray or receive the Eucharist through neglect or indifference . . . (Pause)
ALL: Lord, open my heart to desire You more.
LEADER: Zaccheus was open to Jesus' presence and that was grace . . . For the times I've closed my heart to Jesus' presence in my neighbor or in the needy (the poor, the hungry) . . . (Pause)
ALL: Lord, open my heart to your presence.
LEADER: Zaccheus examined his life and became aware of his sinfulness and that was grace . . . For the times I've avoided self-examination by escaping into work, or pleasure or excessive leisure or by refusing to look at myself in quiet and prayer . . . (Pause)
ALL: Lord, open my heart to my own sinfulness.
LEADER: Zaccheus made a complete change in his life and accepted Christ's forgiveness and healing love and that was grace . . .

For the times I did not admit my own failure to my spouse, children or friends, and for the times I neglected God's healing love in the sacrament of reconciliation . . . (Pause)

    ALL: Lord, open my heart to sincere conversion.

    LEADER: Zaccheus made amends over and beyond what was necessary and that was grace . . . For the times I failed to make amends for my sins of dishonesty, cheating, slander, and lying and for the times I failed to have a sincere purpose of amendment . . . (Pause)

    ALL: Lord, open my heart to a sincere purpose of amendment in order to heal the effects of my sin. (Pause for further private examination.)

IV. Sign of Sorrow: (*Remain kneeling*)

"My God, I am sorry for my sins with all my heart. In choosing to do wrong and failing to do good, I have sinned against You, whom I should love above all things. I firmly intend, with your help, to do penance, to sin no more and to avoid whatever leads me to sin. Our Savior, Jesus Christ, suffered and died for us. In his name, my God, have mercy."

V. Symbolic Action of Reconciliation and Absolution:

(*Be seated until it's time for you to come forward*)

A. First, the penitent comes forward to the priest who asks: "Will you open the door of your heart?" The penitent then responds "I will" and then confesses.

B. The priest gives absolution, or if a non-sacramental penitential celebration is used, the priest imposes hands on the penitent's head after asking the question of the penitent.

C. Then the penitent goes to the assisting minister on either side to receive the symbol and returns to the pew.

VI. Sign of Peace: (*Stand*)

Before announcing the sign of peace, the presider comments on the symbol: "Salvation has come not only to the individual, but to this house." Then he comments on the meaning of the sign of peace. Song: "Father of Peace" by Michael Lynch (Raven).

VII. Common Penance: (*Please kneel*)

Recite together:

"Let us thank the Father, Son and Holy Spirit for . . .
Salvation has come to your house today.
Let us praise the Father, Son and Holy Spirit for . . .
Salvation has come to your house today.

Let us worship the Father, Son and Holy Spirit for . . .
Salvation has come to this house today."

VIII. Concluding Song:

Sing: "Praise The Lord My Soul" by John Foley, S.J.

Suggestions:

1. The sanctuary could have a stage prop of a door with trees on the side. In the Holy Family Reconciliation Service, we used the talents of a parishioner who made a wall and an open doorway with cloth drapes hanging over the doorway. Behind the drapes, we printed a large-shaped heart on poster-paper, bearing the words, "Salvation Has Come To Your House Today." The drapes were opened up after the confessions.

2. The symbol given out after the absolution was a 5 ¼ x 4 ½ inch card that is folded into the shape of a door. On the outside were the words "Look, I stand at the door knocking," and on the inside was a smaller version of the heart described in suggestion one, with the words, "Today, salvation has come to this house." (LK 19:9)

3. Mime was used as a way of reinforcing the gospel story as it was read.

4. The following songs could also be used in this service:
"For You Are My God" by John Foley, S.J.
"Yahweh, The Faithful One" by Dan Schutte, S.J.
"All the Ends of the Earth" by Robert Dufford, S.J.
"Answer When I Call" by John Foley, S.J.
"By Name I Have Called You" by Carey Landry
"Song of Abandonment" by Carey Landry

Part V
Themes for Creating Your Own Services

MORE THEMES AND SYMBOLS

Introduction

Although we have presented sixteen complete reconciliation services, we realize that all of them are subject to modification, depending on the resources available and also depending on the needs of the penitents you are ministering to. But this chapter challenges you to go further than just modify the services.

Using the following skeletal ideas, we invite the pastor, the liturgist or liturgy committee, the retreat master, youth minister or religion teacher to create his or her own communal reconciliation. We suggest the theme and symbol and occasionally a Scripture text, but the rest is left to the creativity of the reader.

Most of the themes and their symbols were possible reconciliation services of the future, services we ourselves one day wanted to construct. It is left up to your imagination to take the themes and construct a communal reconciliation that enfleshes the theme in every way, including a symbolic gesture by the penitent.

I. Theme: Renewing the Covenant With God

Symbol: *Marriage Vows*

The Bible is a love story of God's covenant or marriage with his people. From the creation story on down through the ages, God chose a people as his own. In the story of the Israelites, idolatory was seen as adultery (e.g. Hosea), or the breaking of the marriage bond with God. In the New Testament, through Jesus Christ, the covenant is extended beyond the Jewish people to all people. A Christian's sinfulness is also seen as a form of idolatry and infidelity to the covenant — a choosing of someone or something over God Himself. In this reconciliation service, the marriage vows (or a modification of them) could be used to renew the covenant between the congregation and God. The priest or a leader could represent God in renewing His love and faithfulness to the people; the congregation could then renew their vows to God. The renewal of vows could come after the absolution.

II. Theme: Heal Our Blindness

Symbol: *Loaf of Bread:*

This reconciliation service builds on the Gospel of Luke — the story of Emmaus (Lk. 24-13-50). The disciples were blinded to the meaning of Scripture and its promise as well as to the true identity of the stranger. In John's Gospel, Jesus often refers to sin as blindness. Because of our rationalizations, our refusal to look at the needs of others (note the meaning of the parable of the Good Samaritan) we also sin. Like the disciples of Emmaus, we close eyes and ears to the meaning of Scripture and the promises that Jesus attaches to the Eucharist.

The symbol for this service could be small loaves of bread to be taken home to share with the family, or people could be invited to a post-service gathering of bread, cheese and beverage. The bread must be broken and shared to emphasize that, in breaking, Christ continues to be present in the Eucharist and in our neighbors.

III. Theme: Judge Not, For We Too Have Sinned

Symbol: *Sand*

This reconciliation service builds on John's story of the woman caught in adultery. Instead of condemning the woman as the Law and the Pharisees were prone to do, Jesus in some way mirrors back to the Pharisees their own sinfulness. According to some commentators, Jesus was doing more than doodling in the sand; He was actually revealing the hidden sins of the accusers. We do not come to this service to point fingers at others, but rather to take a look at our own sinfulness. Jesus reveals his compassion for all people regardless of how serious their sins might be.

The symbol for this service is sand. A large shallow box filled with sand could be placed in a prominent place in church. As a gesture indicating their own sinfulness, the penitents would be requested to draw a line in the sand prior to their confession of sins.

IV. Theme: Jesus Gives New Life and New Freedom

Symbol: *Resurrection Plant or Seed Taped to Cloth*

This reconciliation service revolves around John's account of the resurrection of Lazarus. Jesus came not just to give new life to Lazarus, but also to remove the burial wrapping which impeded his freedom of movement. Likewise in the sacrament of Reconciliation Jesus comes not only to give us God's grace of New Life, but also to help free us from the compulsions of sin, the fetters of sin.

Here there could be two possible symbols, a seed taped to a small piece of cloth. The seed would symbolize New Life; the burial cloth, New Freedom. The resurrection plant would be an optional symbol for this service. When placed in water, this seemingly dead plant comes to life. Individual samplings of this plant could be given as a take-home to each penitent so that they could experience the wonder of New Life. If the plant is used as symbol, the homilist should emphasize that the sacrament of Reconciliation was often referred to as a second Baptism by the early Church Fathers.

V. Theme: You Are the Salt of the Earth

Symbol: *Salt*

The success of this theme depends heavily on the way the homilist handles the topic of salt. Because of medical warnings, salt today has some negative connotations. In Jesus' time, salt was a precious preservative and the principal way of flavoring food.

Jesus called on the Christian to preserve the human values of the Gospel in the midst of a sinful world. He also asks us to give flavor and zest to life by living out the hope-filled message of the Gospel. In the pre-Vatican II ritual of Baptism, salt was used to represent Jesus' call to become salt for the world. A small amount of salt can be put in a cellophane container and blessed before giving it to each penitent to remind him/her or his/her call and mission.

VI. Theme: We Are Restored to New Life in the Second Adam (Jesus) and the Second Eve (Mary)

Symbol: *Apple*

This reconciliation service would be a good one for Advent. The theme is that humankind finds a new beginning in the Second Adam and Eve. The service centers on a French folktale which, for theological reasons, has been modified. The story unfolds this way: "Not revealed in the Scripture is the visit at Bethlehem to the Christchild and Mary by a very ancient couple. Their only gift to the Christ child is an apple. The story reveals that the ancient couple is Adam and Eve coming to the Savior for forgiveness for their sin in the Garden of Eden. As they give the gift, they are blessed by becoming young and vital once more."

The apple is the basic symbol in this service. Each penitent receives an apple as they enter church. They will return the apple to attending ministers before the absolution as a sign that their sins have been forgiven and they have been renewed in Christ, the second Adam.

VII. Theme: Advent and a Call to Conversion

Symbol: *Washing Hands*

The theme for this service must include the gospel story of John the Baptist calling us to repentance. John's mission is to call a people to conversion so that they might be ready to receive salvation from Jesus the Messiah. John's baptism is a baptism of repentance. Water thus becomes the dominant symbol for this reconciliation service.

As at the end of the offering of gifts at Mass and as a symbol of cleansing, the priests washes his hands in preparation for the coming of the Savior in the form of bread and wine. So, too, the penitents are invited to do the same symbolic gesture in preparation for the absolution and coming of Christ the Savior. Several servers may be necessary to allow this washing to happen smoothly.

VIII. Theme: He Was Put to death for Our Sins

Symbol: *Hammer*

The theme for this reconciliation service reiterates the ageless truth that sin is not just a private act. Every sin affects other people. In that sense, Jesus not only dies because of the sins of the Romans or the Jews, but also because of the sins of humankind. A wooden cross is placed in a prominent position in the sanctuary. The penitents are invited to take a hammer and pound the cross as a sign of their participation in the crucifixion of Jesus. The hammer thus becomes the dominant symbol of the penitent's guilt and sinfulness. Obviously, this theme would be most appropriate for the Lenten season, but could be used for other times as well.

IX. Theme: Christ Helps Us With Our Shadow Self

Symbol: *Masks*

In the West, we speak of the seven capital sins; in the East they refer to the nine basic compulsions, our shadow side. (Refer to the Sufi Indian Enneagram concept.) In Western spirituality, we are seen to have a basic dominant weakness. In Eastern thought, we are seen as having a shadow side of our personality which needs first to be acknowledged, then dealt with and finally healed.

This reconciliation service could center on the seven capital sins or the nine compulsions of the Sufi wisdom. The purpose of the service is to unmask our dominant sin or compulsion and ask Christ to draw us toward healing and wholeness. The basic symbol for this service is the various masks by which we cover up our sins or weaknesss. This idea could well serve for All Saints Day, using Halloween masks and/or mime to illustrate sins or compulsions.

X. Theme: Jesus, Light of Forgiveness, Removes the Darkness of Our Sins

Symbol: *Candle*

John's Gospel especially makes Jesus the Light of the World. Jesus is not only the Light revealing the identity of the Father, but He is also the Light, in direct opposition to the darkness of sin. In this reconciliation service, Jesus comes to reveal the compassion of the Father and also to reveal our own sinfulness and to be a healing Light for our darkness.

The basic symbol for this service is the lighted candle. The Easter candle could hold a place of prominence in the sanctuary. If possible, the church atmosphere should exemplify the dark/light contrast. As a symbolic remembrance, a small candle could be taped to a card on which a quote from Christopher Movement could be used. "It's better to light one candle than to curse the darkness."

XI. Theme: Letting Go Of Our Sinfulness

Symbol: *Nickel*

The theme of this reconciliation service would center on the idea of letting go of things which attract us, feed our selfishness and prevent our openness to God and to others. A nickel is given to each penitent as he or she enters the church. The coin represents not just our poverty, (sin is often very shallow and superficial) but also the pleasures and talents God has given us for our use. When we grasp these things for our own selfish pleasures (contrary to the will of God), we often misuse God's gift of life, the body and mind. He gives us the material things for our growth and development. The homilist can emphasize the above ideas and the coin can be returned or let loose in a symbolic gesture of the penitent's willingness to let go. The assigned penance could focus on using one's talents or material gifts to enrich the lives of others.

XII. Theme: More Than Crocodile Tears

Symbol: *Oil*

True conversion is more than hypocritical and shallow *tears in the eyes*; it involves *tears in the heart*. Likewise, true conversion in the heart leads to action and service to our neighbor.

In the Gospel story of Luke 7:36-50, a sinful woman finds Jesus eating in the house of a Pharisee. She not only had tears of repentance, but washed Jesus' feet with those tears and then anointed them with precious oil. Her conversion led her to offer Jesus a service of hospitality that had been omitted by a self-righteous host. She overcame human respect in order to offer Jesus a gesture of respect and love.

The story of Luke's would be an interesting one to mime. The homily could point out the contrast between the pride of Simon and the humility of the sinful woman. The examination of conscience could focus on our own areas of insecurity. The annointing of the penitents' hands after the absolution could be connected with some common penance involving service to his/her neighbor.

XIII. Theme: Die to Self and Be Saved

Symbol: *Ashes*

The theme of this reconciliation service is that new life can come from death. The ashes not only represent death to our own selfish and sinful actions and desires, but they also represent the potential of new life. The legend of the Phoenix Bird can easily illustrate the theme. The Phoenix in burning itself to ashes gives birth to a new life. This is a symbol of the Paschal Mystery, the mystery of death and resurrection in Jesus. The relationship of this service to Ash Wednesday is obvious. If possible, a fire could be started at the beginning of the service so that ashes could be available for signing each penitent during the service.